PRAISE FOR THE GUIDES FOR THE PRAIRIE GARDENER SERIES

"The Prairie Gardener's series offers knowledgeable yet accessible answers to questions covering a broad range of topics to help you cultivate garden success. Get growing!" —Lorene Edwards Forkner, gardener and author of *Color In and Out of the Garden*

"This is a beautiful and incredibly well-written series of books on earth-friendly gardening. Lavishly illustrated, with photos in every segment, the books are a pleasure just to leaf through, but the accessible writing and level of expertise makes them essential to any gardener's library. Although they're geared to prairie gardeners, I found great information that transfers anywhere, including where I live, in the Sierra Foothills, and will enjoy them for years to come. Well-indexed, to help you find solutions to elusive problems. Highly recommended!" —Diane Miessler, certified permaculture designer and author of *Grow Your Soil!*

"All your gardening questions answered! Reading the Prairie Gardener's series is like sitting down with your friendly local master gardener. Delivers practical guidance that will leave you feeling confident and inspired." —Andrea Bellamy, author of *Small-Space Vegetable Gardens*

"The Prairie Gardener's Go-To series comes in mighty yet digestible volumes covering popular topics like seeds, vegetables, and soil. These question-and-answer styled books get to the root of the matter with Janet and Sheryl's unique wit and humor. Although each guide touches on regionally specific information, the wisdom of these seasoned gardeners applies to any garden, wherever it may be." —Acadia Tucker, author of *Growing Perennial Foods*

T0017107

JANET MELROSE &
SHERYL NORMANDEAU

The Prairie Gardener's Go-To for

Perennials

TOUCHWOOD

Copyright © 2023 by Janet Melrose and Sheryl Normandeau

All rights reserved. No part of this publication may be reproduced, stored in a retrieval system, or transmitted in any form or by any means, electronic, mechanical, photocopying, recording, or otherwise, without the prior written permission of the publisher. For more information, contact the publisher at:

TouchWood Editions
touchwoodeditions.com

The information in this book is true and complete to the best of the authors' knowledge. All recommendations are made without guarantee on the part of the authors or the publisher.

Copy edited by Warren Layberry

Proofread by Meg Yamamoto

Designed by Tree Abraham

Photos by Janet Melrose and Sheryl Normandeau with the following exceptions: p. 39 (Arina P Habich / shutterstock.com), p. 86 (courtesy of Andy Schalk), p. 89 (Adny / shutterstock.com).

CATALOGUING DATA AVAILABLE FROM LIBRARY AND ARCHIVES CANADA

ISBN 9781771513920 (print)

ISBN 9781771513937 (electronic)

TouchWood Editions acknowledges that the land on which we live and work is within the traditional territories of the Lkwungen (Esquimalt and Songhees), Malahat, Pacheedaht, Scia'new, T'sou-ke, W̱SÁNEĆ (Pauquachin, Tsartlip, Tsawout, Tseycum) peoples.

We acknowledge the financial support of the Government of Canada through the Canada Book Fund, and the province of British Columbia through the Book Publishing Tax Credit.

This book was produced using FSC®-certified, acid-free papers, processed chlorine free, and printed with soya-based inks.

Printed in China

27 26 25 24 23 1 2 3 4 5

Dedicated to all prairie gardeners

Introduction

Welcome to the world of perennials! What's in a name? After all, William Shakespeare once wrote, "That which we call a rose / By any other name would smell as sweet,"[1] which is, of course, true. But humans love to pigeon-hole things with names—for good or for bad—and in the plant world, names seem deliberately designed to bewilder, misdirect, and confuse. So, for the purposes of this book, we need to specify at the outset which types of plants we are dealing with in this very broad category of "perennials."

By definition, the word "perennial" is something that is "lasting a very long time or happening repeatedly or all the time."[2] In botany, perennial generally means a plant that lives for three or more years. (Annuals are those plants that live only one year, completing their entire life cycle in one season. Biennials are those that do so within two seasons.)

Perennials are usually categorized as woody or herbaceous. Woody refers primarily to trees and shrubs, whose hard stems contain lignin. Herbaceous perennials have more pliable stems that contain cellulose.

If we want to get even more technical (and we do!), herbaceous plants can be further divided into graminoids, those that are grasslike, and forbs, broadleaf flowering plants.[3] (Just for fun, the category of forbs includes not just perennial plants but annuals and biennials, too.) There are weeds that are perennial, as well as forage crops, herbs, bulbs, and many more.[4]

In this book, we are going to include only desirable (for our gardens) species whose aerial structures (stems and leaves) die back to their crowns each fall, but whose roots remain alive, though dormant, throughout the non-growing months. Oh, and naturally, they need to survive and thrive in our northern, highly variable, temperate climate. We are primarily focusing on gorgeous perennial flowers (and we'll show you some photos containing some serious eye candy), but we'll also cover a generous selection of perennial vegetables that can be grown on the prairies.

This mixed planting truly epitomizes a "go big" style. Magnificent!

We think that leaves us with lots to talk about, don't you? And that's exactly what we're going to do! In *The Prairie Gardener's Go-To for Perennials*, we'll cover how to select perennials for your garden and get them growing—from stratifying and sowing seeds to transplanting and dividing. We'll give you some tips about how best to water, fertilize, mulch, and deadhead them. We'll help you diagnose and treat problems that may arise and discuss how to tackle challenging environmental conditions. Above all, we'll give you the information you need to make your perennial garden as successful as you can while promoting biodiversity and creating a healthy habitat for pollinators and wildlife. Why not dig in?

—SHERYL NORMANDEAU & JANET MELROSE

Do perennials live forever?

Check out any old homestead on the prairies and chances are that there will be a peony and rhubarb plant or two still thriving. Maybe some hollyhock and even a tangle of 'Jackmanii' clematis. We could be entirely forgiven for thinking that all perennials live for what seems like forever.

Herbaceous perennials have an advantage over annual plants, as they use a lot less energy flowering, fruiting, and maturing seeds for reproductive purposes—something in the order of 20 to 30 percent less than annual species.[5] That's a lot. What the plant mostly does with that energy is grow bigger root systems, enabling it to have more stems, foliage, and flowers every year.

Some perennials, like peonies, are very long-lived, but all have a natural lifespan determined by their genetics and the growing conditions they encounter. Some are considered short-lived perennials that last three to five years. Short-lived perennials typically produce a lot of seed each year; those in the Asteraceae family (daisies and asters) are good examples. All that seed production takes its toll on them, and they simply do not re-emerge one spring. Some, such as hens and chicks (*Sempervivum tectorum*), will flower once they have accumulated enough energy to reproduce, but then the "hen" dies after being completely spent. All is not lost, though, as each "hen" will have grown lots of "chicks" or offsets, continuing the species. After all, *sempervivum* is Latin for "forever alive."[6]

Happily, if planted in the right place, with the right soil, and with ongoing care from the gardener, most of our common perennial species will adorn our gardens for quite a while, getting larger each season with all those glorious blooms.—**JM**

Given proper care, peonies will remain our garden friends for decades.

Plant Selection

1

Species, variety, cultivar, and nativar: What's in a name?

First a bit of terminology. A species can be defined as "a type of plant having certain characteristics that differentiate it from other members of the genus, and which retains these distinctions through successive generations."[1] Often we see a "native species" mentioned to indicate that it belongs to a range of habitat where we live. A plant that is native to other ranges is an exotic or introduced species when grown in our own gardens. A "variety" is a subset of a species that occurs naturally and whose seed will come true to type, for example, *Dictamnus albus*, which has white flowers, and its pink variety, *Dictamnus albus* var. *purpureus*. Incidentally, the genus *Dictamnus* has only two species, of which we commonly see the one species and its variety.

"Cultivars" (short for cultivated varieties) are those where humans have bred something that doesn't occur in nature. While some cultivars have simple parentage, others have a very complicated lineage. Generally, cultivars are grown to enhance a particular trait—or trait of their parentage—such as habit of growth, size of mature plant, colour, and size of flowers, whether they bloom continuously or all at once, and so on. They are largely propagated asexually as their seed will not breed true to type. Due to the amount of work required to develop the cultivar, they are often patented.

Lately "nativars" are appearing; they are cultivars of native species, bred to have certain characteristics of the wild species to be more appropriate for the garden. They are also more readily available as collecting seed from native species in the wild must be done very carefully so as not to exhaust the natural supply of seeds.

We also hear the term "hybrid" tossed around to differentiate between the original species and those that have been bred through cross-pollination of different species. In the context of common use of terminology, a hybrid is the same as a cultivar. A cultivar is what has been bred through the process of hybridization.[2]

Complicated, isn't it?—JM

12

*Pink gas plant (*Dictamnus albus *var.* purpureus*) is a variety of the white species.*

Should I plant species and varieties or cultivars?

There is no simple answer to this question as the variables that will influence your choices are manifold.

Here are the pros and cons for each choice:

Species and varieties are those that can be propagated by seed as well as asexual methods, a real advantage for gardeners who enjoy self-sown seedlings or collecting seeds. They often have a long history of growing well in a particular habitat. I speak from many years' worth of buying perennials, and it is my experience that the original species are often hardier than the fancier cultivars. *Often* but not *always*, as some cultivars have enjoyed as long a life as the species in my garden. Species and varieties are usually magnets for pollinators, beneficial insects, and sometimes those that are our native pests. Their blooms carry bountiful pollen and nectar. If fragrance is part of their tool box to attract those pollinators, it is there in full force. However, some species and varieties may not be as well behaved in our gardens as we would like, sprawling and flopping over, not to mention straying out of bounds.

Cultivars are bred to improve performance and be more attractive to us gardeners than their ancestors. For instance, many dwarf cultivars are bred to be shorter or have a better branching habit, with the flowers being much the same as the species, which can be better for smaller gardens. Others are bred to have bigger flowers, in different forms and hues, and possibly longer bloom times, all characteristics that are appealing to gardeners. There is considerable research being undertaken these days as to whether the different appearance of cultivars means that native insects and other wildlife get confused and will not or cannot recognize them, either as food sources, shelter, or hosts for breeding.[3] While it appears that most cultivars will attract more or less the same attention as the original species, those that have significant changes to their blooms—especially double and triple forms instead of single forms or those more cluttered with petals— can perhaps frustrate or inhibit insects from finding their way into the pollen, and that is a concern. Some cultivars simply do not have significant pollen and nectar, which can create starvation for visiting life. Sometimes cultivars do not produce viable seed, assuming that they have been fertilized, which reduces food sources for birds. On the other hand, cultivars, of both introduced and native species, may have better resistance to our native pests and may also be better adapted to changes in the climate.

A larger issue may be that cultivars, bred asexually, are genetic clones. With the current imperative for rebuilding genetic diversity within species, this is problematic, potentially giving rise to a reduction of disease resistance and degradation of species genetics.[4]

Also of consideration are possible impacts for native species should cross-pollination occur between cultivars in our gardens with those in the wild, especially if loss of viability of seed is a consequence. Our gardens are not isolated, and the ability for seed to travel great distances by wind, water, and animal is a reality, and we cannot foresee potential unintended consequences that may result.[5]

So, this is not a straightforward choice, and the advice of experts as well as our instincts are our best guides. I have a mix of both in my garden, but I avoid the cultivars that are really fancy versions of the original because I figure if I don't recognize it for what it is, then no other life form will either.—JM

Should I plant native perennials or stick to those that are bred for being in gardens?

One of the great debates in gardening in this century is whether gardeners should choose native species over exotic species for their gardens. While the debate can be polarizing, the reality is more nuanced, just like nature itself.

A native species is usually defined as one that evolved in a certain geographical region over time and has not been influenced by human agency. Often a timeline is used such as the arrival of Europeans in the New World. A non-native species is one that was introduced by mankind either by accident or intentionally after that arbitrary line in the sand. Over time an introduced species can escape cultivation and become naturalized in its new environment to its benefit or detriment. Dandelions are a prime example of naturalization. An invasive species is often categorized as an introduced species that is capable of significantly altering the natural ecosystem, often by outcompeting the native species there.

Native species are promoted as being better for our gardens as they are adapted to our climate and native soils and thus are hardier, require less water, are able to withstand pests, and require less maintenance and care. They are also preferred as native fauna have co-evolved with them and recognize them as sources of food and shelter.

Exotic or introduced species are often presented as being the opposite. Further, some are able to outcompete native species, go on to unbalance natural

This naturalistic garden design boosts biodiversity in the landscape.

ecosystems, and reduce biodiversity. It is true that there are many horror stories of exotic species introduced as being desirable ornamental plants, including creeping bellflower (*Campanula rapunculoides*), which was introduced to the prairies more than a century ago. However, the number of invasive species is an estimated .01 percent of introduced species.[6] Many that naturalized have actually added to the total biodiversity of ecosystems, creating their own niches.

While it was presumed that our native micro-organisms and animals would not recognize non-native species, research has shown that the opposite is true. Our native insects, birds, and animals are quite as happy to feast off and forage on exotic species as on native species, so long as they are generalists and do not require specific hosts.[7]

The argument becomes even more nuanced when we consider that nature is always evolving, responding to changes in the environment. A native species, such as the mountain pine beetle (*Dendroctonus ponderosae*), can become a pest and wreak considerable damage to an ecosystem. Our native white yarrow (*Achillea millefolium*) in a garden setting, with its rich soil and plentiful water, can become an outstanding pest. Throughout the millennia, species have spread by way of wind, water, animals, and, in the case of human agency, through migration, warfare, exploration, settlement, and trade. Once in a new environment, arriving species have adapted to it, as the native species have adapted to them.

In naturalistic planting design, the emphasis is not on the argument of native versus exotic species. Rather, it is how best to create plant communities and garden ecosystems that are links to the natural landscape.[8] It is more about recombinant or designed plant communities that are biodiverse, using both native and exotic species to create gardens that are arguably no longer native environments, be they urban or rural settings that promote biodiversity and wider ecological benefits.[9]

So, not a simple answer to a simple question at all. There is so much research to enlighten us and, yes, change why and how we garden, including the plants we choose to be part of our gardens. In assessing my own garden, I have realized that it has evolved over the years to become its own community, embracing both native and exotic species in equal proportions and home to a wide assortment of wildlife. I have chosen them with care for how they will fit into the garden and contribute to the whole.[10] —JM

How can I build biodiversity in my garden with perennials?

Biodiversity is literally the web of life, with species from all the kingdoms represented, be they plant, animal, or micro-organism. One of the greatest challenges to biodiversity in any ecosystem is the loss of habitat for any and all species, which is contributing to mass extinctions throughout the world. The good news is that as gardeners we are able provide habitat for many species through the way we design, plant, and care for our gardens.

Variety is the spice of life and never more so than when it comes to the perennials you choose for your garden. Include as big a range of species in the garden as can comfortably exist within the environmental conditions and design for your garden. That doesn't mean one of everything all higgledy-piggledy, which will drive you and the wildlife crazy. What you are looking for is a range of species that occupy different niches in the structure of the garden, such as tall architectural ones, middling-sized ones, and low-growing, ground-hugging ones. Look for different flower forms, from those that are easy to land on, such as *Echinacea*, to tubular *Delphinium*. Plant different colours: blue and yellow attract bees and white attracts moths. Consider perennial species that have fragrances to attract pollinators or perhaps pungent aromas to repel certain insects. Especially important is selecting species that bloom at different times of the season, from the earliest spring flowers such as *Hepatica* and creeping phlox (*Phlox subulata*) to the last to leave the garden such as Japanese anemone (*Anemone hupehensis*) or Joe Pye weed (*Eutrochium purpureum*). The goal is to have a constant supply of food by way of nectar and pollen throughout the entire growing season. Another consideration: choose perennials with seed heads or fruit that will provide food for birds over the winter or perhaps provide nesting sites.

Our perennials serve other functions beyond providing nectar and pollen. Many can also be larval hosts for butterflies and moths. That means that, as caterpillars, they will be munching their way through foliage, so be prepared for some holes, though seldom do I notice much damage in my garden and it's never as bad as the mess the red lily beetle makes of all our lilies.

This garden bed is a pollinator's dream!

Our perennials provide shelter from wind, rain, cold, and heat. Just as we may place our delphiniums where the wind won't knock them over, our hostas out of harm from hail, or our ligularias out of the heat and sun, we can place others in spots that will provide shelter and breeding spots for visitors.

The goal for us as gardeners when we seek to build biodiversity in our gardens is to create a safe, secure, and inviting environment for all that dwell in it. For me that includes my cats carefully treading their way along the paths, a skunk or two meandering through the growth, and every organism—micro or macro—that cares to visit or make it their home (within reason—I draw the line at moose). Perennials make it easy for us to do this![11]—JM

Is hardiness zone important when selecting perennial plants?

When growing perennials, you'll need to know the hardiness zone of your area. You expect your perennial plants to survive winter and come back (hopefully) year after year. Hardiness is a measure of how well a plant is able to do that. Hardy plants should be able to handle adverse winter conditions; tender plants will not. (Notice that I said *should*—plants are alive and there are so many factors influencing their survival that even if they are rated as hardy, they sometimes don't make it.)

When you head out to the garden centre and are faced with all those zone numbers on the plant tags, you need to know how to make the match between the plant and your garden's particular zone. Fortunately, we don't have to do all this science ourselves—the government has done it for us. Canada's plant hardiness zone designations were created by Natural Resources Canada, and you can easily find a map of them online. The hardiness zones take into account criteria such as minimum winter temperatures, maximum summer temperatures, precipitation, wind, and elevation to arrive at a zone rating for every location in the country. There are nine zones, with the mildest being 8. There are two subzones for each zone, as well: a and b. Zone b is milder than zone a. In Calgary, where I live, we have a hardiness zone of 4a. That means that zone 4 plants should successfully overwinter in my garden, as should plants that have hardiness zones of 0 through 3. I shouldn't expect any plants with a zone 5 rating or higher to be able to overwinter in my garden. (Sometimes, if you can create or utilize microclimates in your garden, you might be able to overwinter a zone or two higher, but it doesn't always work.) When you go shopping, look at the label on that lovely perennial you are eyeballing and match the hardiness zone to that of your garden. In my case, I want that label to say hardiness zones 0 to 4.

Bear in mind that the United States doesn't have the same hardiness zones we do. They operate under the USDA (United States Department of Agriculture) system, which has eleven zones and considers only minimum winter temperatures as its criteria. This means that if you are looking online for plant hardiness zones, you need to adjust for the difference.[12]—SN

20

Should I plant multiple plants or single plants?

Traditional design theory emphasizes the way we view objects. In gardens, there is often a large plant or a very interesting species, one that commands our attention. The rule of odd numbers continues this theme as ones, threes, and fives are seen as dynamic. Essentially, odd numbers make for tension as they are not balanced (except as a triangle). Even numbers are just that, even and balanced, and our eyes see them that way. Often odd numbers of plants are viewed as an informal planting whereas even numbers lend themselves to being more formal. Six plants of the same species have a bigger impact but are better separated into two smaller groups, providing for repetition and echoing of a design. Seven or more are a drift or mass planting depending on the shape that they occupy in a bed. Their sheer number makes for a large impact.

Wildlife gravitates to different plants and parts of the garden, and we can see different patterns in the way they move and interact within the space. A single plant among many different others can get lost, unvisited and unfertilized. Insects tend to flit and flutter between masses of similar plants. They take shelter in the foliage and lay their eggs. That doesn't necessarily mean a single species needs to be mass planted, though that is effective. It can also mean repetition throughout a bed, interspersed between other species.

Consider, as well, that plants are social organisms, forming communities of older plants and new seedlings and supporting other life forms. They fill all the niches of the landscape, each according to their needs, with each species balanced in a tapestry of life. They protect each other from pests, provide support physically and form symbiotic relationships, occupy different root zones, share resources, and sometimes politely or not so politely compete for them.

All these perspectives matter when it comes to choosing plants for a garden. We can plant single plants of any species—plant collectors do this all the time! But if you can, balance those focal points with others that are planted in groups and layers. We know we have got it right when everyone who is and should be in the garden is healthy and enjoys being there.[13] —JM

Pondering, Planning, and Planting Your Perennial Garden

2

What types of root systems do herbaceous perennial plants have? Why does this matter?

We often focus on the top parts of a perennial. Flowers and foliage are what often guide our choices for the garden bed. But it's my view that the type of roots a perennial has is the most important factor (besides whether the species will actually survive and thrive in the garden). If the plant isn't root hardy for our climate, then its roots are moot! Roots govern how the species grows. The roots dictate whether the plant will behave, staying in its spot and slowly increasing in size over the seasons, or growing rampantly throughout the bed, creating havoc wherever it goes.

We need to know if this one must find its forever home the first time it's planted because if you try to relocate it, it will sulk at the very least but more likely go toes up. Or will it be happy to be dug up, split up, and spread about at the drop of a hat?

The type of roots will often tell us if it will be drought tolerant even in hot, dry soils, or if it is going to need consistent moisture in the top few inches, or even if it really wants to be almost submerged.

Roots also inform us gardeners as to the best methods and most successful ways to propagate the plant, be it by seed, cuttings, layering, or division.

The root systems of perennials typically fall into three major categories. Species with taproots have a large, long, central, often fleshy root that goes deep into the soil with the entire root system forming a tight clump. A few lateral roots may branch out from the main root and the root system taken entire is usually closely intertwined and dense. The system stores a lot of energy as carbohydrates and can reach moisture from way down in the subsoil. These species often are long-lived and drought tolerant and thrive on neglect. They hate to be relocated, divided, or otherwise mucked about. On the positive side, they stay put where you put them. Just give them lots of space to grow in girth and everyone is happy. Species with taproots include peony (*Paeonia* spp.), gas plant (*Dictamnus albus*), balloon flower (*Platycodon grandiflorus*), lupine (*Lupinus* spp.), bleeding heart (*Lamprocapnos spectabilis*), false blue indigo (*Baptisia australis*), columbine (*Aquilegia* spp.), bugbane (*Actaea* spp.), and dandelion (*Taraxacum officinale*).

Balloon flower has significant taproots that make it difficult to transplant.

Some perennials have woody taproots rather than fleshy, such as lavender (*Lavandula* spp.), Oriental poppy (*Papaver orientale*), and Russian sage (*Salvia yangii*) and other *Salvia* species. They are equally unhappy with being disturbed once established.

Many perennials have fibrous and shallow roots spreading out from the mother plant. Daughter plants develop from shoots growing from the roots with each offset being part of the larger clump. They do not have a central or main root, tap or otherwise. These species will gradually outgrow their space, with all the daughters competing for resources, but not necessarily go wild about town. Those relatively shallow roots mean that they have moderate drought tolerance, love to be mulched, and require a steady hand on them to keep in good order. The good news is they aren't fussy about being dug up; they divide naturally into separate plants and re-establish quickly. These are easily the most numerous species in our gardens and include purple coneflower (*Echinacea purpurea*), hostas (*Hosta* spp.), primroses (*Primula* spp.), rudbeckia (*Rudbeckia* spp.), summer phlox (*Phlox paniculata*), and so many more.

A subset of perennials with spreading roots comprises those with stolons growing along the soil above ground and runners that grow underground. Strawberries come immediately to mind with their above-ground stolons, but think of those spreading geraniums (*Geranium* spp.) and snowdrop anemones (*Anemone sylvestris*) with their roots running below the surface. Those with roots on the surface include some stonecrop (*Sedum* spp. or *Hylotelephium* spp.) and some just below the surface such as bee balm (*Monarda* spp.) and bugleweed (*Ajuga reptans*).

Finally, there are the species with rhizomes, which are really modified underground stems. They act similarly to the fibrous-rooted species, with the rhizomes spreading abroad from the original plant. Roots and shoots can grow from each node in the rhizome, making them prolific in growth. The ability to grow new plants from portions of the stem gives them a real advantage for survival in adverse conditions. In terms of their behaviour, some species are very well behaved such as iris (*Iris* spp.) and elephant ears (*Bergenia* spp.) as they slowly increase and have shallow roots. Others are the bane of any garden in the wrong place, as they are extremely aggressive in their growth. Lily of the valley (*Convallaria majalis*) and goutweed (*Aegopodium podagraria*) can be a nightmare, but the one that takes the cake for me is bouncing bet (*Saponaria officinalis*), whose roots went a full three feet (one metre) deep and took me three years to remove from the garden bed!

So, before you buy or accept as a gift any new perennial, be sure to learn a bit about its roots. Everyone involved will be thankful you have done so![1] —JM

Do the roots of clematis really need to be kept cool as everyone claims?

Clematis aren't overly happy in hot, dry soil, so yes, this advice is true for them. The recommendation that always follows this is to plant a ground cover perennial to shade the roots of the clematis. If you have enough room so all the plants are not competing too heavily for space, water, and nutrients, then that may work, but adding a layer of two inches (five centimetres) of mulch, such as shredded leaves or bark, around the base of the clematis is a decent alternative.[2]—**SN**

Happiness is a mulched clematis plant.

What sunlight requirements do perennials have?

Perennials have a huge range of sunlight requirements, which are almost always determined by the conditions of their native habitat.

The seedlings sold in garden centres are often labelled to reference the amount of sunlight needed in order to thrive. If they are a flowering species, this can reflect the optimum energy they need to have to form buds and bloom. If plants are placed in lower light conditions than they prefer, or the other way around, then the size they should grow to is often diminished, as well as the size of leaves and flowers. Foliage and flower colours may be modified. Plants may also be less healthy, leading to incidences of pests and diseases that impact them profoundly.

Generally, if a species is labelled as requiring full sun, then you are looking for a site that receives at least six hours of direct sunlight. It needn't be a continuous stretch, so if a tree for instance blocks sunlight for a few hours in the middle of the day but the plant gets morning and late afternoon sun, that works. Partial sun is deemed to be four to six hours a day, with some at least in the afternoon when the light is most direct. Partial shade is the same amount of sunlight as partial sun, but the bulk of the sunlight the plant receives should be in the morning when the light is softer and more at an angle than overhead. Full shade is conditions where less than four hours of sunlight is received, and most of the time it is diffuse light. Dappled light is for those perennials planted under deciduous trees.

It gets tricky, though, given our northern latitudes where the sun's path across the sky changes by the day, meaning a garden or bed or even just a corner will receive differing quality of sunlight as the season progresses. The other factor to the sunlight we receive on average is its greater intensity given the higher altitudes where we garden. Living in Calgary, with its bright, high-intensity light, I only plant full-sun perennials if they are really suited for that blast of light. I am cognizant as to whether their foliage, in particular, is able to handle it. So, in my south-facing bed there are yarrow (*Achillea* spp.), artemisia (*Artemisia* spp.), lavender (*Lavandula* spp.), Russian sage (*Salvia yangii*), and so on. Catch me placing lungwort (*Pulmonaria* spp.) or ligularia (*Ligularia* spp.) there? Not a hope.

Yarrow is content to be sited in a south-facing bed.

Should you live close to large lakes, the light changes with the diffuse clouds that arise with daily evaporation. Pollution in cities changes the quality of the light, as does smoke from wildfires.

On the other hand, often perennial species are labelled as needing more shade than they might need, because full sun often means drier soils. Give those so-called shady plants soil that really retains moisture, and they can handle and even flourish in that extra sunlight. Marsh marigold (*Caltha palustris*) planted with its roots in the damp soil of a pond is a perfect example.

Most of our perennials can readily handle partial sun to partial shade. It is the extremes where we have to be really careful about the light quotient. Our perennials will usually tell us whether they are happy where we planted them with lots of flowers and gorgeous leaves. If they are sulking, then it is time to see if there is a bit better spot to relocate them.[3] —JM

Why are some perennials sold as shade-loving plants?

Not all perennial species are full-sun lovers. Planted in sunny and often hot locations, their leaves will often exhibit leaf curl, sunscald, or browning edges, signifying their displeasure. Some will wilt excessively even though there is sufficient soil moisture. Lungwort (*Pulmonaria* spp.), leopard plant (*Ligularia* spp.), and bugbane (*Actaea racemosa* syn. *Cimicifuga racemosa*), just to name a few, will look like they are on their last legs only to magically revive the moment they are back in the shade.

Most species that have evolved in shadier conditions, be they woodlands or in multi-layered canopies, have larger but thinner leaves than their sun-loving cousins. They also contain more chlorophyll, which can move around within their leaves so that every chloroplast works to catch the sunlight that reaches them. These species are more efficient in harvesting sunlight and storing it away for times when there are lower levels of sunlight. Think of those perennials that love dappled shade. Most of their yearly photosynthesis occurs before the trees above leaf out. This is also why some shade-loving perennials are ephemerals, disappearing come summer when they have used up their energy reserves, only to reappear the following spring.

Most shade lovers also prefer soil that is more acidic along with the moisture and higher organic matter that are typical of woodlands and alongside waterways and boggy areas. They are adapted to the nutrient values found in these soils.

The interesting thing is that the adaptations that our shade lovers have for low light conditions happen during leaf development. Once leafed out, they cannot change, should light levels alter.[4]

The other interesting thing is that often perennial species are designated as shade lovers when growing in much different climatic conditions than we experience on the prairies, including light levels, relative humidity, maximum temperature, and soil types.

What that means is that—while I hesitate to plant full-shade species such as foamflower (*Tiarella cordifolia*), wake-robin (*Trillium grandiflorum*), and certainly not our tall bluebells (*Mertensia paniculata*) in the harsh sunlight—I am more than up for siting species that actually prefer more sun out in the open. The proviso is that the soil is amended to be especially moisture retentive and protection offered from the full blast of sun while they are getting established and developing extensive root systems. I was sold when I saw Joe Pye weed (*Eutrochium* spp.) thriving on a south-facing slope one year![5] —JM

What soil is best for perennials?

Perennials vary in the type of soil they require from almost straight-up sand to bog heavy clay. To complicate matters, some species prefer acidic soil (pH less than 7), and others need alkaline soil (pH greater than 7). To be perfectly frank, it is easier to choose your perennials for the type of soil you have rather than trying to have soil amended to match their needs. Less cost, time, and energy, and ultimately less frustrating.

However, the good news is that most of the perennials we commonly have in our gardens are fairly easygoing as to their soil requirements. Primarily what they need is moisture-retentive, well-draining soil. Although that sounds like an oxymoron, it ensures that their roots won't drown or rot in waterlogged soil nor suffer from lack of moisture. Your soil should be reasonably fertile. It should not be rock-hard clay that inhibits good root growth.

When creating a new bed, prepare your soil with lots of compost, perhaps manure if you have a trusted source, peat moss or coir fibre, and amendments, such as zeolite to further loosen heavy clay if you are blessed (cursed?) with that type of soil. If you know your soil is depleted of nutrients, this is the time to incorporate fertilizers into the soil mix. (We talk extensively about amendments in *The Prairie Gardener's Go-To for Soil*, so we won't go into more detail here.)

Once the soil is prepared and allowed to settle for a bit, you have a broad canvas with which to work, and you may start designing and planting the perennials you wish.

You can't simply sit back and admire your handiwork, however, as soil microbes and macro-organisms will chew through the organic matter in the soil in no time at all. Because perennials are, well, perennial, they stay where they are for years at a time, and you won't be wanting to disturb the soil and their roots. To continually improve your soil's texture, structure, and fertility, annually side-dress the soil around your plants with a layer of compost, about an inch or so (2.5 centimetres). It will get incorporated into the underlying soil through the action of soil life, and nutrients will slowly seep down through the soil profile. Keeping a layer of mulch on top, such as leaves or shredded bark, will also aid the process as it slowly breaks down over the seasons. Because I have heavy clay soils, I also will sprinkle zeolite on top every so often where it will slowly work its way down into the soil to do its work.

For those perennials that absolutely demand specific soil types, it is relatively easy to locally amend the soil where they will be located, even if it is a mixed bed. For those ones it is best to prepare the soil to specifications ahead of planting, and then keep it that way through annually top-dressing the soil with the needed amendments.

Better still, if you have space and the desire, create a bed or garden area with soil and moisture requirements absolutely suited to species with very specific requirements. From bogs to alpine crevices, having the environment best suited to them will provide the ideal conditions for them to thrive.[6] —JM

Can I grow perennials in containers?

Why not? So long as you are prepared for some extra work to ensure that they will come back next season, perennial containers can be a welcome change up from annual containers. Not only that, but you save yourself from having to buy new plants each season. You can also treat yourself to some perennials that have really specialized growing conditions. Or for those of us who hanker for something right out of our zone, a container can be the best choice, so long as you have a plan for overwintering. I enjoy the challenge and the results!

The first consideration is the containers themselves. Perennials have larger root systems, so choose the biggest container that will work for the space it will occupy. The container must have drainage to avoid oversaturated soil that will lead to anaerobic conditions at the bottom and the problems that brings. Choosing an inner container to go into a larger container that doesn't have drainage holes can be a choice for sure, but make sure that water doesn't simply accumulate within the outer container. If the container—plants and all—is going to stay outside planted up all year long, then it needs to be strong enough to handle the freeze/thaw action throughout winter.

When choosing your plants, select those that have similar light, moisture, and nutrient requirements. Soil is not so much of a consideration, as a soilless growing medium will be required instead of garden soil for all but very large containers. Choose species that are at least one to two zones hardier than your area if you are going to leave them in their containers outside all year round or overwinter the container in an unheated garage. Those roots must survive in above-ground conditions where cold will penetrate through the bottom and sides of the container.

For the most part, species with clumping or fibrous roots do better in containers than those with fleshy and/or rhizomatous roots that will quickly outgrow any container. When designing the container, bear in mind that, because the root systems are necessarily constrained, the perennials you choose may not attain their normal size at maturity.

Perennials seldom have extended flowering periods, so the ones that are best suited for containers will have interesting foliage, texture, or habit of growth beyond their blooming time. A good tip for perennial containers is to design for the foliage, with the flowers as the secondary interest.

At the end of the season, you will need to consider overwintering methods. I take apart the container and transplant my perennials in a nursery bed for the winter, early enough that they have a chance to settle in and then well mulched in for the months ahead. But then I don't have a garage, which can be a good choice if you wish to leave the perennials in the container over winter but are worried that their roots will be damaged. If that choice is not available, and there is no room in your beds, then grouping all the containers you have together on the ground, with a mulch such as straw for insulation around the containers, and well covered, may work. It all depends on the winter and how variable the weather turns out to be. In chinook country, I don't dare try this option. Finally, there is the choice to leave them *in situ* in that very large container with enough soil to protect the roots. But for the super-tender, out-of-zone perennials, they must come inside.[7] —JM

We encourage experimenting with growing perennials in containers!

Occasionally, you can get perennial plants such as this rhubarb to overwinter successfully in a container.

The Care and Keeping of Your Perennials

3

Should I start perennial flower seeds indoors for transplanting later in the spring? What is the best way to go about doing this?

The biggest thing to realize when starting perennials from seed indoors is that they usually take a very long time to germinate, and then they grow slowly. These plants do not take off like annuals—which makes sense, given that they don't complete their life cycle in a single growing season. Annuals are speedy because they need to be. Some perennials can take months to germinate, so patience is a necessity.

Some perennial seeds will need to be cold stratified before sowing. (See page 40 for instructions on how to do this.) Factor in the time it will take to accomplish this when you determine how far in advance of spring you should sow your perennial seeds. Your seed package will help you with the math and tell you how many days to germination, as well as suggest how many weeks before transplanting outdoors that you should sow the seeds indoors.

You can choose to use a commercial seed-starting or potting mix or create your own (one recipe—of a myriad—is made up of equal parts of coir or peat moss and perlite or vermiculite). If you have a propagator tray, go ahead and use it, but any container will do. We prefer plastic over peat containers, as the latter dry out quickly (and if you use peat pellets, you have to contend with that horrid mesh afterwards). You can always reuse plastic when it is properly cleaned.

Sow your seeds into damp, not waterlogged, soil. Make sure the seeds have good contact with the soil. Some plants need light to germinate, so don't cover those seeds. (We have a helpful list of which plants need light to germinate in *The Prairie Gardener's Go-To for Seeds*, page 40.) Don't bury the seeds too deeply or they may have difficulty germinating.

There is no need to fertilize your newly sown seeds; they have all the food they need stored up in the endosperm of the seed itself.

Cover your seed trays with a dome lid or a clear plastic bag. You do not want to see a huge amount of condensation forming, as this can lead to mould issues. Remove the lids if everything starts getting a little too moist.

Place the seed trays in a warm location, out of direct sun. You can use a heat mat if you wish, but it's usually not necessary. If you choose to use a heat mat, run it for only a few hours each day and remove it once the seeds sprout.

Once germination occurs, pop the trays into sunlight or under your grow lights. Keep the young plants watered (but not too wet) and make sure they have excellent air circulation. (You can run a small fan nearby just to give the plants a bit of a gentle breeze.) Once the plants have obtained approximately three to four sets of true leaves, you can start fertilizing them every two weeks or so. Use a sparing amount of compost (if your potting mix doesn't already include it) or a water-soluble synthetic fertilizer such as 20-20-20.[1]—SN

A lovely sight: freshly sown trays of perennial seeds!

Do I need to stratify my perennial seeds before planting? How is this done?

Many perennial species that have their native ranges in northern temperate regions require a period of moist and cold soils to germinate. It makes sense, because they wouldn't want to sprout in September, only to die as winter arrives. Perennial species native to tropical regions have not evolved to require this period of chilling, called stratification. We naturally gravitate to those species that will overwinter in our gardens because we aren't crazy about replacing multiple plants every year. The result is that most of our common perennial species require stratification. Their seeds contain many germination inhibitors such as abscisic acid and waxes and oils that break down over the winter months until finally the seeds are ready to germinate, coincidentally just about when spring arrives.

The easiest way to stratify perennial seeds that you have collected, or that you know have not been sold pre-stratified (the packet should tell you if they have been so treated), is to direct sow them into the garden or in pots in the fall. Make sure they are well marked so that you don't forget what you have sown and where—they will come up in spring when conditions are right for their germination. I use a cold frame for pots, placed out of the sun and wind, and stuffed with straw or burlap sacks so that temperatures are buffered, and the pots do not dry out readily.

If you prefer to sow them indoors so that you have seedlings to transplant, then the refrigerator will be needed. Seeds are stored dry, with a moisture content below 10 percent. They need to increase that moisture content before the process of breaking dormancy can take place, so presoak them in water for up to one day. Then place the seeds in either damp vermiculite or potting soil in baggies and put them in the fridge for a minimum of a month. Some species need longer, so it is wise to check beforehand for the recommended time requirements. Once ready, they can be sown into pots to germinate. Or if you left it a bit late, you can always direct sow them into the garden as soon as the soil has thawed, but while air temperatures are still cool.

If they don't germinate, do not fret. Don't disturb them for the year, and there is a good chance they will germinate next year after going through winter.[2] —JM

Patience is required when sowing perennial seeds! These stunning peony seeds can take up to three years to germinate.

Should I direct sow perennial flower seeds? If so, when is the best time to do it?

Absolutely! Nature does it for us all the time with bountiful results. My garden is filled with volunteer perennial plants from western columbine (*Aquilegia formosa*) to forget-me-not (*Myosotis sylvatica*) to snowdrop anemone (*Anemone sylvestris*) and more, each with its different method of seed dispersal. Sometimes I find new plants in totally different locations in the garden and even between the flagstones.

What most of our common perennial species require is a long period of stratification, anywhere up to four months or more, and luckily the prairies provide that to us regularly! They also, more frequently than, say, our common edible seeds, require specialized aids to break dormancy, such as scarification or even alternating periods of wet/cold and dry/warmth. Generally perennial seeds take longer to germinate than other seeds. Peonies are a great example as they can take up to three years to germinate![3] All of which leads us to believe that we are really chancing our luck to deliberately direct sow perennial seeds, what with the various conditions needed to break dormancy, not to mention the life in the garden, from ants to birds, consuming them.

The best technique for deliberate direct sowing that I use for special species is to dedicate part of a nursery bed to the exercise, using a cold frame system to provide some control of chance factors such as the dratted squirrels. In fall, I will sow seeds I have either collected or obtained from reputable sellers, after first researching for extra information for their treatment. For instance, one of my favourites, false indigo (*Baptisia australis*), needs to be scarified first.[4] Then I mark each seeded spot with a plastic marker as some species have irregular germination, and I don't want to get impatient and disturb them. Gas plant (*Dictamnus albus*) is one for sure![5]

After sowing, I often place row cover over the soil surface, then mulch with compost to protect the seeds from the variable temperature cycles of winter that Calgary experiences. (In areas with winter-long snow cover, that step isn't necessary.) In spring I easily remove the mulch without disturbing the seeds below.

Allow the seedlings to grow in the cold frame all summer, and those that are ready can be transplanted in fall. Some, like my gas plant, I leave in place for a couple of years so that they are stronger before they go into their forever homes.

I don't use this technique for all perennial species I want to grow from seed. I let prolific plants do their own thing and move them around as needed. Some are easier to propagate indoors. Some, such as *Rudbeckia* species, are great to direct sow using cold frames as they germinate readily, grow quickly, and can be transplanted in early summer. But for those long-term propositions, the satisfaction that comes with success can't be beat![6] —JM

How do I know that my perennial plants need to be divided?

Perennials are like people. We all need the tough love treatment every so often!

Make no mistake, dividing perennials, especially ones that have become monsters, is a lot of work. It is also a lot of disruption for the plant, so not to be done at a whim.

An indisputable time is when said perennial is growing too big for its britches, crowding into other plants and elbowing them out of the way. Time to cut it back to size and give it and the others more space. While you are at it, consider whether it should be there in the first place, or in your garden for that matter. Repeatedly doing the same task over multiple seasons always smacks to me of a form of insanity.

While some perennials remain happy and prolific forever, it seems, without your help, others will decline after a while, exhibiting smaller leaves and weaker stems, and producing fewer blooms every year. Others naturally die out in the centre with the younger growth around doing the heavy lifting of blooming. Rejuvenating these species is kind to them and they always respond with renewed vigour. We gardeners hate to consign a plant to the compost heap, but discard the older portions that are tired rather than attempting to keep them going. The younger portions will re-establish beautifully, but those old ones will struggle.

A school of thought is that it is time to divide when the plant looks its best. It's healthy, vigorous, and a good size. So long as it is large enough to divide into three to five portions, then why wait until it is in decline? You are practising proactive management of your garden along with greatly increasing the number of plants you have. This is a particularly good practice if you are wanting to fill in your garden with species you love without having to buy more, not to mention being able to share the bounty with friends and strangers.

Finally, be sure that the perennial in question is one that wants to be divided. Not all species enjoy the experience, and some will either sulk for ages or just go to plant heaven to your profound dismay.[7] —JM

44

When is the best time of the growing season to divide perennials?

It depends on you, your climate, and your perennials. The old adage is that if a perennial blooms in spring, then you divide it in fall. Likewise, those that bloom in fall should be divided in spring. The sound reasoning behind the maxim is that you do not want to disrupt a plant that is devoting a lot of its energy into growing buds and flowering with the need to repair its root structures—besides, any plant that has been divided is going to feel poorly for a bit and looks a little ragged around the edges. Summertime has traditionally been avoided due to the heat stress that would be placed on divisions, which have fewer roots to draw up moisture.

There is another school of thought that says that any perennial can be divided once it is finished flowering. For the remainder of the season, it won't be actively growing, and some go into dormancy. It can be a good time to take advantage of the cycle of that species and divide then. Oriental poppies (*Papaver orientale*) and globeflower (*Trollius* spp.) are good candidates for that immediate attention once they have flowered and before they disappear. Often the new divisions will reappear come fall for a late summer growth of foliage and maybe a flower or two.

We should also consider our specific climatic conditions, as to when our plants are best divided. Winter leaves northern latitudes slowly, and our soils stay cold and often saturated well into spring. Some years our perennials are correspondingly reluctant to stir, with new growth only coming in come May. There isn't much time to divide them and have them settle in before the heat of the season is upon them. On the other hand, at the tail end of summer our soils are warm and dry and the nights are getting cooler. Yet there are still some weeks (months?) of the gardening season left for those divisions to snuggle into the soil and get those roots moving, without the need to grow new leaves and buds.

On the other hand, in late spring it is easy to see where the natural divisions are in the crown, with growth just emerging. There is less rough handling of stems and foliage. Plus, there is the undeniable fact that, in spring, the plants have the most stored energy in the roots to aid in re-establishment.

But consider, too, when you will have the time to care for new divisions, regardless of the accepted wisdom. If you know that you are going to be too busy to nurture them, then don't divide. I generally do most of my dividing in that sweet spot after the heat of the summer with a weather eye to the sky and the long-range forecast. But that timing generally matches the cycle of my available garden time and energy. Just because it is ideal for me, doesn't mean it works for you.

There are a few perennials, though, that absolutely must be divided in fall, primarily those with dense and/or fleshy roots, such as hollyhock (*Alcea* spp.), or those that set new growth buds (eyes) in fall, such as peonies (*Paeonia* spp.).[8] —JM

Feel free to divide globeflower after it has finished flowering.

How do I divide my perennial plants?

The word "division" sounds so daunting, doesn't it? It's not! Here is an easy, simple guide to dividing your perennial plants:

If you are able to do so, water the plants that you want to dig up the day before you do the deed. Damp soil will make your job much easier, and it will lessen the stress on the plant somewhat.

Grab that spade or garden fork! Dig up the plant in a clump, being very careful to get as much of the root ball as you can. Try to minimize the damage as much as possible.

Gently remove the excess soil from the root ball with your gloved hands. Doing this gives you the chance to inspect the roots for any signs of girdling, rot, or other issues. It also facilitates the actual task of division.

With a sharp knife or the edge of your spade (depending on how large the root ball is), cut the crown (base) of the plant apart. This may require some strength on your part. Do as little damage to the roots as you can. You want each clump to have an excellent chance of successfully re-establishing itself. Look for "eyes" or growing shoots on the roots and separate the clumps so that each clump has about three to five active shoots on it.

Dig some holes for your new plants. The hole should be as deep as the root ball and twice as wide. Lay the newly divided clump into the hole and backfill it with the soil you've removed. There is no need to amend the soil at any point during transplanting.

Water the plants well and keep up with a regular watering schedule while the plants re-establish themselves. Hold off on the fertilizer until the next spring.

If you aren't ready to transplant your divided perennials just yet—for example, you're saving a clump for a friend—put the clump in a container and keep it out of direct sun until it is given away. Water it when the soil dries out but be careful not to overwater.[9]—SN

When is the best time to transplant or divide peonies?

Once peonies are established, they usually don't need to be divided for a good long while (seriously, they can go for decades!), so the decision to divide them isn't one you have to make very often. If you've sited your peonies properly at their initial planting, you likely won't transplant them, either, unless perhaps you move house or want to gift a plant to another gardener (lucky them!). But if the time comes to divide or transplant an established peony, do it in the early autumn, around the first two weeks of September. There is a very specific reason why this is the best time (versus, say, the spring): the tuberous roots of the plant start to form masses of slender feeder roots in preparation for the following year. New growth buds (sometimes called "eyes") also develop on the roots. Winter's freeze doesn't destroy this activity, it simply suspends it, and when the weather warms up again in the spring, the plant kicks back into action. You want to transplant or divide your established peonies just before this occurs so that there is time for the plants to get ready for dormancy.

Because peonies *really* do not like to be transplanted or divided, they will likely show their displeasure by not blooming the following year (sometimes not even the year after that!). Be sure to plant them so that the eyes are just below the surface of the soil, not too deeply or they won't bloom for you. Peonies need time to re-establish those roots, so be patient with them—the wait is worth it! Site them carefully so you do not have to move them, and don't be in a rush to divide them. They simply do not need it.[10]—**SN**

When you dig up a mature peony to divide or transplant it, this is the sight you're greeted with. Those roots are formidable!

When should I cut back perennials—in the fall or in the spring?

Okay, I can't resist! This is truly a *perennial* debate among gardeners!

It used to be de rigueur that we had to go out one day in fall and literally remove all the foliage from our perennials right back to their crowns. That manicured look going into winter was the gold standard.

Then came the alternative. Leave everything up and do it all in spring. The thinking was that the stalks captured snow and gave some protection from the rigours of winter. Those plants with seed heads provided food for wildlife and the rest gave shelter. The only problem with this approach was that come spring— and with our soil cold and wet—we had to wait until the soil thawed and warmed up to get into our beds. By then some of our perennials might be pushing their new growth up through the old. Besides, in gardens with a lot of bulbs inter- planted between the perennials and sending their noses up to sniff the air, there is little room for garden shoes to get in the bed without crushing something.

If you have a large collection of spring-flowering bulbs such as this delightful scilla growing in your perennial beds, you may wish to perform your garden cleanup in the fall. That way, these little beauties can put on a big show for the pollinators (and everyone passing by your garden) during the following spring.

So the debate goes between the fall cleaner-uppers and the leave-it-till-spring-ers.

Over the years I have evolved my approach, with a gradual removal of foliage as it dies back, with the energy gained over summer withdrawing into the roots to better overwinter. Any diseased or insect-infested plant debris ends up in my municipal compost bin, but the rest goes into my compost pile.

Some plants I always cut back—those whose foliage turns to slimy mush over the winter. Hostas, day lilies, irises, and peonies. Yuck. Or the ones that will fall over and create tripping hazards as I prowl the garden in winter.

Any that can provide shelter and food stay up, especially those with hollow stems and great seed heads. Really that is most of them when you think about it. That extra plant matter also protects any that are half-hardy to the prairies.

Some years fall is prolonged, and I might get into the beds and tidy things up a bit more. Some years winter comes early, and nothing gets cut back. Some years I don't even get into the beds in spring and the new growth takes over, and I cannot even see where the old is for the new and it slowly disappears and contributes to the soil.

Which is all to say that our perennials mostly take care of themselves in this regard, and the task of cutting back is largely self-imposed so that our gardens will reflect the vision we have for them. Tidy in fall or messy till spring. The choice is yours and the weather's to make.[11] —JM

Tell me how to properly water my perennial plants. Is there a rule of thumb to follow?

If there is a rule, it's to water when necessary. This may not be the easiest thing to judge, however. If you have just planted your perennials, they will need to be watered deeply and on a regular basis until the roots are established. That may mean you have to water several times a week, depending on the weather. Once most perennials are established, they can usually be watered less often — but again, it depends on the weather. Rainy, cool days mean you don't have to break out the hose; hot, dry ones do. Drought-tolerant or water-wise perennials can handle longer periods without water, but for their best health, you will still need to provide supplemental irrigation if the drought is prolonged. Do a test to determine if you need to water or not: stick the blade of a trowel up to the handle into the soil. If you pull it out and the soil clinging to it is sticky, you can probably wait to water another day or two. If the soil crumbles off the trowel blade and looks dry, grab the watering can.

As with your trees and shrubs, it is recommended to water your herbaceous perennials about 1 inch (2.5 centimetres) each week. You can use the afore-mentioned trowel to do a quick measurement of how deeply you are getting the water into the soil, or you can use a rain gauge (best if the precipitation is natural rather than coming out of your watering can). To promote vigorous and healthy root growth, it is better to water deeply and less often than shallowly and frequently.

Water at the base of the plants, if you can, instead of up into the leaves. This can prevent the spread of certain fungal and bacterial pathogens. Using a garden hose, a watering can, or drip irrigation is preferable to a sprinkler system. Use mulch in your perennial beds to help conserve soil moisture.[12] —SN

Some plants don't need a lot of water to look their best! Catmint is an easy-to-grow, drought-tolerant selection with attractive foliage and blooms and a pleasant minty fragrance.

Should I mulch my perennial plants?

Mulch, how do I love thee? Let me count the ways!

1. Mulch means I don't have to weed as often.

2. Mulch helps prevent moisture loss in the soil.

3. Mulch protects plant roots from extreme temperature fluctuations.

4. Mulch has aesthetic value and can give your garden beds a finished, tidy appearance.

Do it! Many gardeners choose to use wood chips or shredded bark to mulch their perennial beds for good looks and slow decomposition, but there are many options. (We break down mulches in detail in *The Prairie Gardener's Go-To for Soil*.) A two-inch (five-centimetre) layer is sufficient—less than that may not give you the weed-smothering ability you may want. And don't use landscape fabric beneath the mulch. There are myriad reasons why this is a bad idea, but the biggest one is that it negatively impacts soil life.[13] —SN

Mulch: useful and beautiful!

When should I remove temporary winter mulch in the spring?

In Calgary, where we live, applying a layer of mulch to your perennial garden if you don't already have any is incredibly helpful because we lurch through winter on the backs of extreme freeze-and-thaw cycles. They may give us gardeners migraines, but they can inflict serious damage on our plants, as the soil heaves and thaws, then refreezes again. But ... when should you remove this temporary mulch in the spring?

Any plants growing in an area where winter temperatures fluctuate benefit from mulch applied just before winter sets in. It can be a bit hard to make this call. You've all seen the memes on social media about leaving the mulch layer for overwintering insects such as ladybugs to hang out until conditions warm up enough to emerge. Another thing to consider is why you are using winter mulch in the first place—to control the extremes of temperature. If the highs and lows are still see-sawing dramatically, and there is still ice in the soil, wait a little while longer. (If your soil is still partly frozen, you shouldn't be working in it, anyway—you may risk compacting it.) Pull the mulch off when the weather stabilizes (on the warm side of things) and your perennial plants are just starting to poke through.

If you are using autumn leaves as mulch, it's a good idea to remove the soggy carcasses in the spring so they don't start growing mould. You can throw them in the compost bin.[14] —SN

When should I fertilize my newly planted perennial plants and how often? What type of fertilizer should I use?

New perennials do not need an addition of nutrients at the time of planting. There is no need to drop any amendments down the planting hole; just ensure your soil is in as good a shape as you can get it to begin with. (It's always ideal to offer your new plant babies suitable soil conditions right off the bat—why stick them in any ol' dirt?)

New or freshly transplanted perennials can be given a side dressing of approximately 1 inch (2.5 centimetres) of compost a month after transplanting unless you are planting them in the autumn, in which case don't give them anything at all as it may impede their progression into dormancy.—SN

What is the best way to deal with weeds that are encroaching on my perennial plants?

Weeds are plants like any others, but in their quest to become the most successful denizens of your garden (and surrounding area), they tend to bulldoze all over your cultivated plants. They compete for nutrients, water, space, and sunlight—and that's just the mild stuff. In worst-case scenarios, some weeds are considered invasive and harbouring them might earn you a chat with a provincial weed inspector; at the extreme end of things, some weeds can choke out and kill your cultivated plants. To keep your cultivated plants happy, the weeds must go. There are a few ways to make the removal process a bit easier.

1. Weed when the soil is damp. This recommendation comes with a caveat: Wet soils compact easily and the action of you stepping or kneeling on them to weed can be problematic. If you have raised beds or containers, this isn't an issue; if your beds are in-ground, however, try to stay on pathways instead of going into the beds themselves. Wet roots slide more smoothly out of the ground and tend not to break as readily as dry ones.

2. Yank when the weed plants are just emerging. Easier said than done, I know, but if you can catch them before they grow obscenely monstrous roots or try to set seed, you garden is better off.

3. Dig to the centre of the planet (and possibly sideways several miles). I exaggerate ever so slightly, but you do have to go deep. If you have ever had the absolute pleasure of digging up quackgrass, you know what I mean. Be meticulous and thorough.

4. Use the right tool for the job. I know several gardeners who dig weeds out of the lawn with a butter knife they absconded from the kitchen, and that simple tool can work very well! Some gardeners swear by a carpet knife, or they invest in a beautiful Japanese hori hori knife. There are specialized diggers on the market, as well. I also use a trowel for some weeding tasks—it just depends on what I am up against.

5. If you can't get to all the roots quickly enough, trim the flowers off before they produce seeds. This won't solve the problem—you'll still want to dig—but it will prevent a few more potential plants from popping up until you can act. The key is to prevent seed formation, so be timely about this job.

6. Till lighter (or ideally not at all). Tilling can bring deep, dormant perennial weed seeds to the surface of the soil where, much like Gremlins, they suddenly experience the thrill of light and water and wreak havoc on your gardens.

7. Mulch can help. Applying a two-inch (five-centimetre) layer of mulch—whether it is wood chips, straw, or conifer needles—can prevent weeds from popping up (or, at the very least, cause their roots to weaken so they are easier to pull up).[15]—SN

Do I need to deadhead my perennials? If so, how should I go about doing it?

The reasons for deadheading are varied. Most often, the reason we deadhead is because of the appearance of flowers that have finished blooming. We may want to promote further blooms or flushes of flowering, though in many species you can deadhead all you want and it will not encourage a second flush of flowers. Think peonies, irises, or even dainty *Hepatica*. Sometimes, we want to nip in the bud (ooh, those garden puns!) the self-sowing tendencies of certain perennials before they can even start to set seed. I don't bother with forget-me-not (*Myositis* spp.) or Iceland poppies (*Papaver nudicaule*) as they are welcome to sow everywhere. But globe thistle (*Echinops* spp.) gets the treatment when I think of it, as I really don't need more of them, but if they appear, I can always give away the extras. I absolutely remove flowers the moment they are done from my mountain bluet (*Centaurea montana*). In fact, I want to remove the plants out of the garden altogether but that is another story.

Deadheading also promotes stronger root and stem growth as the energy required to develop fruit and mature seed is then used elsewhere. Sometimes that energy is directed toward flowering again as the plants were cheated, as it were, the first time around. Should the species be one that will develop a further flush of blooms later in the season, they will likely do so whether you deadhead or not, but the flush will be stronger, more pronounced, and more beautiful if the old blooms are tidied away. Woodland sage (*Salvia nemorosa*) is a perfect example.

There are also good reasons to not devote the time and energy toward what can be either an enjoyable task or tedious work, depending on your garden personality. You may want the plant to develop seed so you can collect it. Seed heads can look gorgeous, both as they mature and throughout winter. Those spiky globes of purple coneflower (*Echinacea* spp.) and sea holly (*Eryngium maritimum*) are terrific coated with hoarfrost, as are fluffy clematis. The seed heads of peonies, when they open, are absolutely stunning with vivid pinks and purples inside. Even more importantly, seed heads are food for the life that overwinters in your garden.

The technique for deadheading is straightforward. Simply remove the flower and stem back to the next leaf or a lateral bud, cutting the stem just above.

Done correctly, the plant will look groomed and new growth will be promoted. Fingernails are often all you need for soft stems, but those that are thicker or harder will need a sharp pair of bypass pruners or snippers to do the job without damage to the plant. It takes time to single out each stem, and the temptation is to gather a bunch of stems together for one quick hack—but resist the urge. A few, mostly ground cover perennials, beg to be sheared as it would try the patience of a garden saint to do each small stem separately. Creeping thymes (*Thymus* spp.) and creeping phlox (*Phlox stolonifera*) both get cropped off all at once with a pair of shearers back to just above the foliage.

Be selective when deadheading. It should be an enjoyable task, not a penance, and if you just don't get round to doing it, those perennials will take care of things themselves.[16]—JM

Some of the perennials that I grow reseed themselves like crazy. I love them, but how can I keep them from taking over my garden?

Sometimes it is a serendipitous delight when plants reseed themselves in your gardens; other times, especially after you've pulled hundreds of seedlings out for the umpteenth time in a growing season (I'm looking at you, catmint!), it can be a little less fun. The trick is to not blame the plant, nor bash its reputation—it's honestly just doing what it needs to do to reproduce. (It just so happens to be doing a fabulous job!)

Some annual and biennial plants are absolute superstars at reseeding, but many perennials will do the same thing: if you grow columbines, echinacea, or phlox, you know exactly what I mean. The key to managing perennials that reseed is to prevent them from setting seed in the first place. That means that they need to be deadheaded regularly. (If you still want to attract pollinator insects to your perennial flower garden, leave the blooms just long enough for the bees to buzz, then remove them. This relies on your observations in the garden, and your timing needs to be spot-on to remove the developing seed heads, but it's a way to have your cake and to eat it, too.)

Manually pulling up or digging up the volunteer seedlings will also work. If you want to keep some of the new plants to give away, dig them up carefully and pot them up. You can also move them to other areas of your garden. It's an easy way to get free plants![17]—SN

What types of supports should I use to keep tall perennials upright?

If you grow tall or blousy flowering perennials such as delphiniums or peonies, you'll know the anguish: a sudden storm brings high winds or heavy rain, and afterwards, your plants are left bedraggled and horizontal. (Honestly, peonies—especially double ones—don't even need a weather event to flop over. With those heavy blooms, they just do!) Support is needed for many large perennials, and there are several types of assistive devices to choose from, from sturdy wire hoop-and-stake supports, to wooden stakes or bamboo U-hoops, to mesh cages. Some gardeners get creative and design teepee-like set-ups using willow branches and other tree trimmings. The structures can be as decorative or as utilitarian as you want—just look for a style that will work with the plants you are growing. A large peony cage is ideal for its namesake and allows the plants to grow through the top. A metal stake with a ring at the top might work well for lilies or foxgloves.

You may need soft nylon plant ties to help fasten the stems into place (strips of pantyhose work as well!). Twine may be used as guides for linking stakes. In some cases, as long as you aren't constricting the stems of the plants, you may be able to use twist-ties or rubber-coated wire. Never tie the plants tightly to the stakes.

Try to plan ahead and stake your plants before a nasty weather event happens—you'll thank yourself that you took the time.[18]—sn

My perennials are extremely slow to come up this spring. Should I write them off as dead?

Perennials emerge from the soil when the time and temperature are right, not necessarily when we would like to see them. If the soil is too cool, they will stay abed until the situation changes. (I completely understand. When the house is chilly, I feel like doing this, too!) Other factors may influence how slow perennial plants are to emerge in the spring, such as drought (both summer and winter), insect issues during the previous year, a late spring frost, or even old age. Newly planted perennials might not be quick to jump to action in the spring, either. The timing of emergence may depend on the species, as well—some plants such as Joe Pye weed (*Eutrochium* spp.), Russian sage (*Salvia yangii*), black-eyed Susan (*Rudbeckia hirta*), and balloon flower (*Platycodon grandiflorus*) are particularly slow to pop up—they just need that extra time to break winter dormancy.

If you know you have some plants that are typically slothful in the spring, label them in your garden so you know where they are. This prevents you from plopping a new plant in that supposedly empty space. Protect all your perennials with mulch (see page 52 for tips on why and how you should do this). Also, when you are selecting plants at the garden centre, work within your hardiness zone—don't push the limits if you want to be on the safe side. Don't rush to throw down your money on something new, especially if your winter has been harsh. The roots might be stirring but the stems and leaves are not. Some gardeners will recommend putting in a new plant by July if you don't see anything, but I'm a fan of being extremely patient—if you wait a year and nothing makes an appearance, then consider a replacement.[19]—SN

Joe Pye weed likes to sleep in a bit in the spring, so don't fret if it doesn't show up to the party when you think it should.

My perennials are already growing, and there is a late cold snap or hard frost coming. What can I do to save them?

This is such an unpleasant—and uncomfortably common—scenario on the prairies. Try not to panic too much, however. If your perennial plants are properly sited, cold hardy to your region, and established, they should be okay. Yes, they might have potentially serious dieback of the foliage, but the roots should survive. On the other hand, if you have just tucked in a plant straight from the nursery, even if it is the right hardiness zone for your garden, it may not make it as it is not established or hardened off sufficiently to the sudden cold.

You can cover your perennials if you have enough warning and time to do so. Use row cover fabric or bed sheets instead of plastic or tarps if you can. Position stakes or hoops to keep the fabric from touching the plants, if possible, and tack the covering down to the ground to ensure there are no drafts to let in cold air.

If you choose to use plastic, remove it before temperatures heat up, otherwise you will end up with a sweltering greenhouse with no air circulation.[20] —SN

What are some best practices for saving seeds from some of my perennial plants?

Before setting out to collect seeds from any perennial plants, there are a few considerations to be aware of as they will impact your overall success and satisfaction with the results.

Firstly, determine the exact lineage of your plant. Is it a cultivar or hybrid? Or is it a species or variety? Any hybridized plant may not have viable seed as the breeders may have intentionally or otherwise rendered the cultivar to produce sterile seeds. The cultivar may have been trademarked, in which case it is illegal to collect its seeds. At the very least, any seed collected from a cultivar is not likely to breed "true to type," with resulting seedlings not being at all like the parent.

The best perennials to choose to save seeds from are those that are open-pollinated or heirloom species. While natural variations may occur, for the most part, you will be rewarded with seeds that will grow up to be just like their parents.

Secondly, choose the plants you will be collecting from right from the beginning of the season, and take steps to ensure that they will not be cross-pollinated. As soon as the flowers are out, hand-pollinate them yourself by taking pollen from stamens from one bloom and applying it to the anthers of the ones you are wanting to collect seed from. Then enclose the flowers in a muslin bag, cheesecloth, or other lightweight material to prevent any other pollination from occurring by wind, rain, or visiting insects. Though if you have only one species of any given perennial in your garden, you are safe to skip this step.

Then wait for the seeds to mature. You know they are ready when the entire seed head is tan or brown and looking very dried out. Then cut off the seed head and gently place it in a paper bag and allow it to dry further. The goal is to have any moisture in the seeds evaporate so there is no chance for mould to grow on the seeds. Then release the seeds from the seed head, either with gentle shaking or manual removal, and discard the seed head. I sometimes leave this step until January and on a cold snowy day devote an afternoon to cleaning the seeds and packing them away in envelopes for storage.[21] —JM

Can I bring my perennial plants indoors for the winter?

You can, in some instances, but the first question is whether it is necessary. Only tender perennials that are not root hardy for your zone need to be removed from the garden and overwintered in the house, garage, or (if you are lucky) a passive greenhouse. Really tender ones are divas, and they may reside outside in pots over summer but need to come speedily inside when the nights draw in and temperatures drop.

For the most part, we prairie gardeners have learned to our cost what perennial species are hardy for our gardens. These we can and should safely leave where they are without needing to disturb their roots. Because, make no mistake, taking a plant out of its home to be hailed or chewed on, then back inside in a few months to pot or repot it up, along with making sure that it isn't bringing in bugs, pathogens, or critters, is a lot of work. I know because I always have some moving back and forth, and once I didn't do the job properly and ended up with slugs crawling across the kitchen floor come February. The cats enjoyed the new playthings, but it grossed out the rest of the household!

Tender perennials can be overwintered as houseplants, where we are keeping them actively growing. These are mostly tropical in origin and will need to have the light they normally enjoy provided—usually in the form of grow lights of some sort. They will need to receive normal amounts of moisture and be fertilized once late winter creeps around. The goal is to have them survive being inside for the long months before they go back outside. Think bananas!

Ones from northern temperate or subtropical regions should be allowed to go into dormancy for the bulk of the winter months so they rest, conserving energy for next year and keeping to the natural pattern of winter hibernation. They will require a cooler location, ideally in the range of 40 to 50°F (5 to 10°C), and an unheated garage or passive greenhouse is best. Do allow them to die back naturally, drop leaves, and so forth, and keep the soil they are in no more than slightly moist. Covering them with floating row cover or some other insulating material to keep temperatures around them consistent is a great idea, especially if the garage is used to park a car.

64

There are several steps to follow when bringing in those perennials. Remember the slugs?

For about a week—or at the very least a few days—move those perennials in pots into the shade to start the process of getting them used to lower light levels. If they are in-ground, dig them out and remove as much of the garden soil as you can. This action will eliminate some of the potential hitchhikers, and I have gone to the extent of washing off the soil in lukewarm water in a bucket outside. Then pot them up in new potting soil and get them into the shade. If they are in a large planter that can be moved into the garage or greenhouse, then they can stay in that container as the mass of the soil should be enough insulation.

Next, inspect for diseased leaves and for insect eggs. Quarantine them by placing them in floating row cover bags, as they will need to go inside for the nights and outside for the days. This is reverse hardening off as they gradually adjust to the new living quarters. After a couple of weeks, they can go out of quarantine, assuming no problems, and be inside for the winter.

Continue to monitor for problems, but don't fret if leaf drop occurs.

Given the work to bring any plant inside for the winter months, I am very selective as to which ones come in. I have given up trying to bring in any that are really going to poop out by February regardless of the care they receive and stick to high-value ones. What I have been doing more and more as our winters moderate is heavily mulch those out-of-zone perennials, and more often than not they come back nicely come spring. That way I have space to overwinter my bananas that are not even *close* to being perennial in our world![22] —JM

Perennial Vegetables

4

Is it better to plant asparagus from crowns or from seed?

Asparagus takes a long time to grow to a harvestable stage from seed—five years is an expected duration. To speed things up a bit, plant crowns. (Crowns are root systems of plants that have been grown for two years.) This is one veggie that takes its sweet time getting established, but it is absolutely worth it—a healthy patch of asparagus can keep growing and producing for about twenty years, so you can enjoy it for a deliciously long time. Bear in mind that you shouldn't begin harvesting asparagus from your plants until they are three years old.[1] —SN

If you want to keep eating asparagus year after year, let your plants produce their gigantic, feathery fronds over the summer. They're a bit wild looking, but the plants need them to produce energy for the future.

When should I cut my asparagus fronds back?

After a few weeks of delicious eating, reluctantly it is necessary to stop and let the remaining shoots grow for the season to provide energy for the plant. Harvesting for too long weakens the plant and reduces next season's bounty. Soon 4-to-7-foot-high ferns (1.2 to 2.1 metres) will create a statuesque plant for the summer.

Do leave the fronds or ferns standing for the season until they entirely turn brown in the autumn, either naturally dying back as the days grow shorter or killed by frosts. During this process the plant withdraws carbohydrates contained in the feathery leaves to the roots so that the energy will be there for that early spring growth of delicious spears.

The choice then is to leave them standing for the winter to capture snow among the stalks to protect the crowns or to cut them back to the crown and mulch for winter. A deciding factor is often whether asparagus beetle has made its presence felt that season. If you spotted even one, then absolutely cut back the ferns to just above the crown. Asparagus beetle eggs will overwinter on the dead stalks, so bag them right away to be disposed of in the garbage or by burning, or if you have a municipal hot composting system they can go to that bin.

If you remove the fronds in autumn, then mulch around the crowns with a generous layer of compost that will protect them from all that winter throws their way. But if you leave them up because of early snows or to provide snow trapping, make sure to get into the garden as soon as feasible to cut them back before the new shoots appear![2]—JM

Can I grow ferns that produce fiddleheads on the prairies?

Certainly, we can!

Fiddlehead greens are the young shoots or sprouts of certain ferns. They are harvested when they are thick and tightly coiled, when their resemblance to the scroll of a fiddle is the most pronounced.

It is most important to know which ferns are safe for consumption as some contain toxins. In North America, it is the ostrich fern (*Matteuccia struthiopteris*) that provides us much of this delicacy come spring.

Ostrich fern crowns are readily available at garden centres and through mail order. They are easy to grow: all you need is a shady garden area with moisture-retentive soil that is rich in organic matter and on the acidic side of life, and room for the rhizomes to grow and spread each year. If your garden is on the dry side of shady, add plenty of compost and peat or coir each year to boost moisture retention.

Other ferns are also fiddleheads, such as the lady fern (*Athyrium filix-femina*) and American royal fern (*Osmunda spectabilis*) and many others found in their native habitats around the world. Some taste better than others, and still others are local delicacies. Others are to be avoided in the main, such as bracken fern (*Pteridium aquilinum*), which is known to contain ptalquiloside, a chemical compound that causes health problems if eaten to excess.[3]

It is important to store, clean, and prepare fiddleheads properly as instances of food-borne illnesses have been known to occur from their consumption. It is especially important to always clean and cook them carefully—and never eat them raw.[4]

As with all early spring delicacies, fiddleheads are a fleeting enjoyment, as only a few of the sprouts from each plant should be harvested for fear of weakening the plant. Then let them grow for the summer.[5] —JM

Ostrich ferns produce edible (and mighty delicious) shoots in the spring.

When harvesting fiddleheads, know your plant identification! Not all ferns produce edible shoots.

How can I keep my sunchokes and horseradish from completely taking over my garden? I don't want to stop growing them.

Both sunchokes (*Helianthus tuberosus*, also commonly called Jerusalem artichokes) and horseradish (*Armoracia rusticana*) are grown for their edible roots. Although they may be tasty and desirable, both of these plants can be—to put it mildly—hooligans, spreading with a vigour that can be massively troublesome if you are not prepared. Unfortunately, simply digging up the roots isn't the solution to the problem. In fact, doing this can only make things worse, for new plants will sprout from even the tiniest chunk of root. Instead, restrict these aggressive plants by confining them to a single bed, where you don't plan to grow anything else. Another option, if you plan to grow only a couple of plants, is to plant horseradish or sunchokes into a deep, wide container and sink the container into the ground. Don't use clay or ceramic pots just in case the roots break through and escape. Yes, they are that kind of determined!

These techniques work to help control any perennials that are creeping and spreading aggressively in your garden, not just sunchokes and horseradish. Another option is to site energetic plants where the going isn't so easy. This includes planting them in shadier conditions than they like, leaner soil, or where they face stiff competition, such as near spruce trees.

Before planting sunchokes, be aware of their propensity to spread. Fortunately, there are some fairly easy solutions for controlling them.

Another thing you can try (although not with plants where you plan to eat the roots) is to root prune around the plant at least once a year. This is a technique that used to be performed on trees and shrubs but is not so common a practice these days as it did a lot of damage to the root structure of these woody plants. However, used to control rhizomatous roots, it works beautifully. The trick is to ensure that there is enough space around the individual plants within the bed for each to have good root development. Around the aggressive plant—at least a foot (thirty centimetres) from the crown to be safe—insert a very sharp spade at a slight angle to a depth of around ten inches (twenty-five centimetres) all around the plant. If the plant is a ground cover such as creeping Jenny (*Lysimachia nummularia*) and the like, you will need to go only three or four inches (eight to ten centimetres) deep to be below the depth of the roots. You want to be neatly severing any roots that have grown beyond the perimeter. Next sift through the soil beyond the perimeter to extract them from the soil, ideally before they have had a chance to grow into neighbouring plants. A ton of work, but you may find it worthwhile![6] —SN & JM

Is it true that you shouldn't harvest and eat the stalks of rhubarb that have been touched by a late spring frost?

I can't tell you how many times this comes up as a meme on social media in the late spring, but I can put your mind at ease about this potential hazard. If there is a late spring frost and your rhubarb is in the middle of happily producing delicious edible stalks for you, don't panic. But don't go out and harvest a bunch of rhubarb to eat, either. If it's just a light frost (just touching the freezing point), all may be well. If it's a hard frost (dipping below 32°F or 0°C), maybe not so much. Regardless, wait two or three days before checking on the plants. If the leaves are black and mushy and the stalks have gone limp and mushy, which is likely with a hard frost, don't eat them (they'd be gross tasting, anyway, plus that texture—ew!). Throw them in your compost bin. If they are still firm and look as they should, go ahead and harvest them as you normally would.

Whether it is a hard frost or a light one, the plant itself should rebound in time, and any future stalks it produces will be just fine to eat.

And yes, of course you can freeze rhubarb stalks after you have harvested them. (I'm talking about the good, firm, fresh stalks.) They are perfectly edible, not to mention ideal for pies and cakes and compote and . . .[7]—SN

Let's address rhubarb's identity crisis!

We may think of rhubarb as a fruit, but botanically speaking, it's a vegetable. The part that we eat is the petioles, specialized stems that attach the leaves to the rhizomes of the plant. One of the reasons for the confusion is that rhubarb was declared a fruit in 1947 in the state of New York to avoid a specific tax that seems to have been levied only on vegetables. Because we tend to make sweet instead of savoury recipes with it, it's easy to forget it's not a fruit.[8]—SN

74

My rhubarb has produced a massive flower stalk early in the season. Should I cut it off or leave it?

Some people think they're ugly, but I personally adore rhubarb flowers—they have a fascinating architectural form that I find very appealing. When rhubarb flowers early in the season, before we want it to, this is called bolting. It's usually due to factors such as prolonged hot weather, drought, a lack of nutrients, the age of the plant, and even the variety. Honestly, the plant is supposed to flower and produce seeds—that's its actual biological purpose—but we want to harvest those tasty petioles (leaf stalks) and if the plant is popping out with blooms, it isn't focusing on the stuff we as gardeners consider important, which is making us food to eat, as well as storing carbohydrates so that it can make food for us to eat next year. So, yes, if you want plenty of stalks, cut the flowers off when they appear.

When shopping for rhubarb plants, look specifically for bolt-resistant cultivars in your seed catalogues. The tried-and-true standby 'Canada Red' happens to be one example. (That doesn't mean it won't bolt at all, just that it is not as likely to as other cultivars.)[9]—SN

The blooms may look fascinating, but if you want more tasty stalks, remove the flowers from your rhubarb plants.

I forgot to harvest my garlic. What can be done to save them? Will they grow back next year?

There is a window of opportunity to harvest our garlic. Too early and the individual cloves will not have formed properly, and the bulbs may be small. Too late and the bulbs will already have started the process of preparing for next year's growth, severely degrading the quality, taste, and storability of the bulbs.

The sweet spot is when half the leaves have died back, with some still showing green. On the prairies, that can be as early as the middle of July or as late as mid-August. It all depends on when you planted them, when they sprouted in spring, and the weather after that.

It is easy to misjudge, miss, or downright forget to harvest them. I seem to forget a patch every year and only realize it when I brush against the mature seed heads and scatter the bulbils all over the ground. I have a lot of garlic growing accidentally in my very wild garden!

Garlic plants (*Allium sativum*), be they softneck (*A. sativum* var. *sativum*) or hardneck (*A. sativum* var. *ophioscorodon*) varieties, are perennial by nature, but we cultivate them as annuals, digging them up when mature and replanting for further crops. If left to their own devices, once the cycle is complete with that season's top growth dead and all the energy withdrawn down into the underground organs, they enter a period of dormancy. However, soon they stir, with the outer wrappers decaying and the individual cloves opening somewhat like a flower. While we replant each clove separately so that they have maximum access to resources for the best growth, in nature the cloves will regrow together as a clump following the same life cycle.

The resulting bulbs next season are smaller, somewhat like gourmet, baby leek size, but just as viable and tasty. You can harvest them if you like, use a few and replant a few, and likely the following season they will be as large as we desire. Or just leave them be and they will become smaller shoots, like our dense patches of chives. When you need a couple of shoots for supper, you just dig out what you need. Or once again, like chives, harvest just the leaves for a tasty treat. You

Garlic is surprisingly forgiving if you forget it in the soil over the winter.

will also have lots of garlic scapes, assuming you are growing hardneck varieties, which are definitely an exotic treat.

Allowing your garlic to go feral, as I refer to it, fits into the growing movement toward resiliency and self-sufficiency in our local food systems. It also means you never need to buy seed garlic again, unless you want to try a different variety.[10]—JM

What are some ornamental perennials that are also vegetables?

It's funny. As gardeners we love to pigeonhole our plants as ornamental, vegetable, herb, or weed. Yet plants are just plants, and they often cross over into many of our different arbitrary categories.

We all know of the mantra that we should eat our weeds. Dandelions, chickweed, plantain, and so forth. Dandelions for instance are weed, vegetable, medicinal, dynamic accumulator, and the first plant to bloom in spring with a huge nectar load for the pollinators.

So, what about some of our common ornamental perennials found in our gardens being sources of food?

Hostas (*Hosta* spp.) belong to Asparagaceae, the same family as, you guessed it, asparagus. The furled young leaves that spring out of the soil just like their cousin are called hostons. A delicacy in Japan, they are called *giboshi*. More mature leaves can be used like Swiss chard, and the flowers are edible too.

Day lilies (*Hemerocallis* spp.) are another to try as a dish. The flowers are delicious and often stuffed like a pepper and made into a fritter. Yet all parts of the day lily are edible, from young leaves to unopened buds, down to the roots and, yes, the seeds too!

Guess what? Hollyhocks (*Alcea rosea*) are edible from top to bottom too. Often their habit of self-sowing everywhere can be an issue. But dig them up and eat them instead of tossing the unwanted ones in the compost.

Violas, violets, and pansies (*Viola* spp.) are known for their edible flowers, but their leaves and flower buds are also great to add to soups, salads, or a braised dish.

Other noteworthy species include sea holly (*Eryngium maritimum*) with its steel-blue prickly flowers and seed heads, and even more prickly is prickly pear (*Opuntia* spp.) with pads and flower buds equally delicious.

Red-veined sorrel (*Rumex sanguineus*), cousin of common sorrel (*Rumex acetosa*), with its crimson-veined leaves is an early spring green yet often is found in the ornamental bed instead. Likewise, I first encountered Egyptian walking onions (*Allium × proliferum*) many years ago literally walking all over a garden, to the despair of the homeowner. Now they are sought after!

The bane of urban prairie gardens is creeping bellflower (*Campanula rapunculoides*), a truly obnoxious weed that was introduced in the early 1900s as a dead hardy, beautiful perennial. Now it is everywhere and crowds out less aggressive species. Those rhizomatic roots that look like parsnips? Yup, they are edible just like parsnips, and taste as good. The young leaves and delicate flowers are good too. Now, just as with the dandelion, we can really eat our way through them.[11]

As always, there is a caveat. Ensure that none of the ornamental or weed perennials you try have been sprayed with pesticides, especially systemic 'cides that will remain in the soil. The health risks are not worth it!—**JM**

Yes, you can successfully grow these beautiful prickly pear cacti in your garden in many parts of the prairies, and, as a bonus, you can eat them!

Pests and Diseases

5

One of the early books of this series, *The Prairie Gardener's Go-To for Pests and Diseases*, covers many of the common problems that may be associated with perennial plants—after all, critters such as slugs and deer, and pathogens such as the ones that cause powdery mildew, are a bit generalist and really don't care which types of plants they gnaw on or infect. In this chapter, we are going to focus on a few more issues of concern specific to your perennial plants and give you some tips to effectively deal with them.

I am devastated! My lilies are being completely destroyed by the red lily beetle. What can I do?

The pernicious red lily beetle (*Lilioceris lilii*) is likely the insect pest that we hear about most often on the prairies these days. These critters showed up in these parts a couple of decades ago, and our lilies have never been the same since. Unfortunately, they are not exclusive in their dining habits: they also feed on hostas, lily of the valley, Solomon's seal, and fritillaria. Don't worry about your day lilies—they are from the genus *Hemerocallis*, which these beetles leave alone. Lilies remain their favourite meals, however, and they can easily decimate swaths of them in a matter of hours.

Adult red lily beetles sport a gorgeous jewel-like red thorax and abdomen, while the rest of the insect is black. At first glance, you may mistake them for ladybugs, but they have no spots, and their bodies are longer at ¼ inch to ³/₈ inch (6 to 9.5 millimetres). The larvae are seldom seen, as they protect themselves by hiding in black gloopy frass (feces). It's super gross and highly effective.

It is thought that the adults can find the plants—and other beetles—by scent, so just when you think you've got them all, they'll fly over from your neighbour's garden and start in on yours all over again. They fly well and can cover great distances.

Did I mention that the adults can successfully overwinter in the soil, despite our brutally cold weather? In the early spring, they will emerge and immediately

These devilishly handsome insects can obliterate your lily plants in mere hours.

start munching on your lilies that are just poking up out of the ground. They will also lay 250 to 400 eggs on the plants. (The eggs are initially tan in colour and are laid in rows. When they are about to hatch, in 4 to 5 days, the eggs will turn red. If you are lucky enough to spot the eggs, you can wipe them all off the plant in one fell swoop and be done with one generation, at least.) Once the larvae are hatched, they feed alongside Mom and Dad and all the other adult beetles in the vicinity, decimating leaves, stems, and floral buds. If unchecked, the larvae will content themselves in this manner for the better part of a month, then they will plop down onto the ground and nestle themselves inside a cocoon to pupate. Another month later, and more adults will pop out and start feeding all over again.

If they sound difficult to deal with, that's a colossal understatement. One of the most effective ways to control them is to painstakingly remove the adults, the larvae, and the frass from the plants using your gloved hands. We used to recommend squishing them, but some recent research suggests that the critters give off pheromones when they are violently dispatched, which only serve to attract more beetles, so now we suggest throwing them in a bucket of soapy water. It's disgusting and you need to go out every single day to tend to your plants, which over the growing season can get tedious. As well, if you have a lot of lilies, you won't likely be able to make a dent. In commercial operations and public gardens, there are some experiments being done with biological controls, where tiny parasitic wasps (*Tetrastichus setifer*) are released to give the beetles a what for, but we aren't at the stage yet where we can use these on any widespread level in our home gardens. Some gardeners swear by certain chemical controls, but I am hesitant to recommend them due to their potential harm for beneficial insects. Besides, there is little evidence to suggest that any one type of control is entirely successful in the fight against red lily beetles. Not yet, anyway. Plant a wide range of perennials in your garden, and you'll be less likely to experience decimation on a massive scale — by the same token, I am also aware of how devoted some gardeners are to their lilies, and I know how much the plants are valued.[1] —sn

My delphiniums are being munched on by worms. What can I do to save my plants?

Those little ½-inch (1.3-centimetre) green worms you see on your delphiniums, monkshood, and larkspur plants are delphinium leaftiers (*Polychrysia esmeralda* or *P. moneta* var. *esmeralda*), sometimes known as delphinium worms. These eating machines are the larvae of a moth. The moth lays her eggs in the fall on her favourite host plants. The eggs have no trouble overwintering in our climate.

When it comes to controlling these little critters, timing is everything. The eggs hatch in early spring (late April and early May), conveniently at the very same time the plants are emerging from the soil and putting out delectable new green growth. What you need to do is thwart them before they start munching away. When your delphiniums, monkshood, and larkspur plants have reached a height of 6 inches (15 centimetres), shear them down to about 2.5 inches (6 centimetres) above ground. Chuck the trimmings in the garbage, not the compost (in case the worms have already taken up residence). This procedure sounds brutal, but the plants will regrow quickly, and you have just deprived all those little worms of their buffet.

If you miss the window of opportunity to cut back the plants, you can hand-pick the worms off the plants. It's an unpleasant task, but if you are diligent, it works.[2] —SN

If the leaves on your delphinium plants are curling and you can see some tiny green worms on the plants, it's sadly too late to take action for the season. Prepare to tackle these unwanted pests very early in the season.

The flower buds of my day lilies aren't opening properly. What could be going on?

Red lily beetles may not take out members of the genus *Hemerocallis*, but unfortunately, day lilies have their own problematic pest to deal with: the day lily gall midge (*Contarinia quinquenotata*). This tiny fly has been busily attacking day lilies in Europe for decades now but has only recently made its way into North America, likely vacationing in plant tissue brought into the country, which was then sold or exchanged, facilitating the spread of the critter.

So, how do you know if the midges are after your day lilies? The most prominent sign is that the unopened flower buds suddenly swell unnaturally or become misshapen. They won't open fully. This is due to the midge maggots growing inside once the eggs laid by the adult flies have hatched. A single bud can host anywhere up to a hundred tiny crawling larvae ⅛ inch (3 millimetres) long. Blech. And guess what? Once old enough, the little gaffers drop out of the buds onto the ground, then successfully overwinter in the soil. They emerge as winged adults in the spring to start the cycle all over again. Positively delightful.

If you see evidence of the day lily gall midge, remove the affected flower buds, bag them securely, and freeze them for forty-eight hours to destroy the larvae. If you have access to a means of safely burning them, you can do that instead. The buds are safe to compost after freezing, but if you're still nervous, throw them into the garbage.

Purchasing bare-root stock can help prevent the spread of the midge, which can hang out in soil in container stock.[3]—SN

If your day lily flowers aren't opening or start looking weird, these little guys may be the problem. (Photo courtesy of Andy Schalk)

My hollyhock leaves are developing yellow and orange spots. What is wrong?

Chances are you have hollyhock rust or mallow rust (*Puccinia malvacearum*) or perhaps *P. heterospora* showing its first symptoms as the fungal spores invade the cells of your plants. Typical of this large family of rusts, they present with typical bright orange or yellow spotting of plant foliage, followed by the development of rusty-coloured pustules on the undersides of leaves that exhibit dark reddish fruiting bodies. Released by wind, rain, and even your watering, they spread far and wide and can infect any species of the mallow family (Malvaceae), including members of the *Alcea*, *Lavatera*, *Malva*, and *Abutilon* genera. As the disease progresses, the spots enlarge and whole leaves can turn a tan colour or become skeletonized, usually falling off prematurely. In severe cases, the rust can infect plant stems as well. While the rust doesn't often kill the plants, it will disfigure and stunt their growth and over successive seasons weaken them. Unlike many of the rust species—which require two hosts as vectors—*Puccinia malvacearum* and *P. heterospora* are autoecious, meaning that they complete their life cycle within one host species.

Likely introduced to your garden either by infected plants and seeds or literally on the wind from other gardens, it is hard to eliminate once established. The pathogen overwinters in plant debris and possibly the living tissues such as roots.

Good cultural practices are essential to keep it in control. All rusts thrive in hot and humid conditions. Ensure your hollyhocks and other susceptible species are well spaced with good airflow. Place them in full sun with soil that dries easily. Mulch to control potential for splashback from watering and hard rains. Monitor plants for those first telltale symptoms of infection and remove any leaves that are exhibiting spots. Proactively spraying foliage with a mixture that is alkaline to increase surface pH, such as Bordeaux mix, can deter the spores from entering. Copper or sulphur treatments can also work to deter the action before it gets going. Disposal of infected plant debris such as leaves and stems is essential, either in municipal compost bins, by burning, or by deep burying in the soil. Scout for and remove any weeds in the Malvaceae family, such as common mallow (*Malva neglecta*), an introduced species—I do love its very apt botanical name! If these methods do not manage the situation, consider removing all members of the mallow family from the garden for a few seasons to break the disease cycle. Or invest in rust-resistant varieties and cultivars such as Russian hollyhock (*Alcea rugosa*) or fig-leaf hollyhock (*Alcea ficifolia*), which are lovely in and of themselves and not so common. Personally, I love to collect hollyhock seeds from plants I know are disease-free or sourced from reputable seed sellers and, after a suitable period of stratification, sow them indoors in February for a (almost) worry-free show come summer![4]—JM

To keep your hollyhocks rust-free like these, use mulch at the base of the plants to reduce the risk of rain or irrigation water splashing back up into the foliage. The water may contain spores of the fungus that causes rust.

It looks like some of my plants have mould growing on them. What can I do about this?

Botrytis blight (*Botrytis cinerea*), also referred to as grey mould, is a serious fungal disease that can affect nearly every part of your perennial plants, turning the tissues blotchy and brown, or grey and fuzzy. Floral buds and flowers may be harmed as well, and the innermost petals may turn brown. They may be deformed or fail to open. Periods of cool, damp weather cause the fungus to proliferate. If your plants have been damaged by wildlife or hail, for example, or they are already in poor health, botrytis blight will be more likely to take hold. Water from rainfall or irrigation splashes the fungal spores up into leaves and stems, spreading the disease. Wind can also transport the spores.

As the fungus can overwinter in plant debris in the soil, be strict about cleaning up any fallen plant parts throughout the growing season, but especially in the autumn. If you prune away any affected plant parts, place them in the garbage, not the compost, and be sure to sanitize your pruners.

Make sure your plants have adequate air circulation—don't crowd them in the garden. If their growth becomes too dense, prune them to allow the passage of air through the stems.

I'm not keen on applying a whole lot of fertilizer to my perennial plants anyway, but to help prevent botrytis blight, go easy on the nitrogen. An overabundance of lush new growth is too tempting for a fungus to pass up.[5] —sn

Botrytis blight can affect most plant parts, including the flowers.

Help! I have been told I have anthracnose on my peonies. What should I do?

When thinking of anthracnose, I always immediately picture my beans getting dark spots on the pods and becoming mushy, icky things to be quickly disposed of in the trash. But anthracnose is not limited to my beans.

Anthracnose is caused by a whole mess of closely related fungal species—such as *Gloeosporium* spp., which affects peonies—where the fruiting body is called an acervulus. You can often spot them as tiny black dots in the lesions, and when the spores are released, they appear as slimy or gelatinous masses.

Anthracnose typically first makes its appearance as dark-coloured lesions or cankers on twigs, leaves, and fruit. They then become sunken, appearing to be water soaked. The disease moves fast, with entire leaves and stems becoming infected and appearing withered or blighted. There can be multiple rounds of infections throughout the season, especially if the weather is what we prairie gardeners consider hot, which is to say 75 to 85°F (23 to 30°C), and humid with lots of wet days—as moisture is essential for the life cycle of the fungi.

Many of our common perennial plants can be affected by anthracnose, including our valuable peonies. The *Bergenia, Hemerocallis, Hosta, Phlox, Rudbeckia,* and *Sedum* genera, just to name a few, are susceptible to anthracnose.

As with many fungal pathogens, should you discover it on your plants, all is not lost. Removal of affected parts of the plant as soon as you see symptoms appear will go a long way to control it, as does cutting back plants to the crown in fall, for the spores will overwinter on the dead leaves and stalks. Preventive actions include ensuring that susceptible plants are not crowded together, creating those ideal conditions for infection to occur. Do prop up heavy plants such as those magnificent 'Sarah Bernhardt' peonies so that their leaves and blooms are not lying on the soil. Avoid overhead irrigation, and water in the early part of the day so that the foliage has a chance to thoroughly dry before nightfall. Finally, if any of your plants were infected last season, you may care to apply a sulphur- or copper-based fungicide to the foliage as soon as the weather conditions appear to be conducive for a repeat this season.[6]—JM

Why are the flower buds of my peonies failing to open?

Peonies sometimes form buds that fail to open (and eventually turn brown or black and shrivel up) due to the fungal disease botrytis blight (see page 89), or occasionally because of the presence of root nematodes in the soil. More often than not, however, the causes are abiotic. This means they are cultural or environmental in nature, not associated with a pathogen or a pest. Watch for factors that influence bud blast and, if you can, try to combat them for lush blooms. Things to look out for include:

* Cold temperatures just as the flower buds are developing. The new buds may never grow larger than a couple of centimetres in diameter, and later in the season, they'll simply turn brown and drop off. There isn't a whole lot you can do about the weather, but you can help protect them by growing the plants in a location away from frost pockets.

* Not enough sunlight. Peonies are not shade denizens, so site them properly for showstopping flowers that fully open.

* Prolonged dry conditions. Peonies don't take well to drought, so ensure they have enough supplemental irrigation when there isn't sufficient rainfall.

* Not enough nutrients. Peonies in lean soil will be less likely to produce their fabulous blooms. Side-dress the plants with vermicompost or compost every spring.

* Plants are not well established. New peony plants or those that have been recently divided are slow to develop their extensive root systems and may experience bud blast in the meantime.[7]—**SN**

Fortunately, this 'Karl Rosenfield' peony isn't experiencing bud blast.

How can I prevent root and crown rots?

All of a sudden, your previously healthy plant is exhibiting wilting foliage that is turning yellow, red, or even purple. You may see dry rot or lesions on stems near the soil line, with stems showing tan or dark patches. You may realize that the plant had stunted growth and perhaps sparse flowering beforehand.

There is a good chance that a soil-borne pathogen has taken hold. Root and crown rots are not just a single pathogen, but either bacteria, fungi, or possibly nematodes that have entered the plant through its roots or potentially through wounds on stems just above the crown at soil level. By the time you see the above-ground symptoms, the roots are disintegrating due to rot.

The culprits are often *Rhizoctonia solani, Fusarium* spp., and water moulds (*Phytophthora* spp.). All are able to survive in the soil for long periods of time without a host. As there is little to do but remove the dying plant, preventing the conditions or environment for the pathogen to take hold is key.

These pathogens flourish in heavy, wet clay soils. They also take advantage of stressed plants, particularly those that are crowded together and where foliage remains damp or wet throughout the day.

Steps to take once the pathogen is present are to immediately remove all affected plants as the pathogen can spread quickly. Some resources recommend sanitizing the soil, but any chemical so applied to kill the offender is guaranteed to affect all soil life. Do, however, sanitize any tools or equipment used to remove the plants.

Amend the soil in the area, ensuring good drainage prevails. In areas that are naturally wetter, consider raising the level of the bed. Add a lot of organic matter to boost soil nutrients and drainage. Reduce the amount of mulch on your beds if the soil is too moist underneath. Consider your techniques and delivery of irrigation. If using overhead water, consider surface irrigation. Avoid overwatering by checking soil moisture before irrigating.

When buying new plants, ensure they are healthy ones from a trusted source to reduce the chance of importing a pathogen into the garden.[8] —JM

Should my rhubarb leaves be turning bright red in the middle of summer?

Rhubarb is not susceptible to a great number of pests and diseases, but one issue that can crop up is red leaf disease, caused by the bacterium *Erwinia rhapontici*. If your rhubarb plants are showing signs of rot at the base (crown) of the plant, and deep brown abscesses in some of the stems and other tissues, be on the lookout for further confirmation of the spread of the disease, such as blackening of tissue in the crown and dieback of the centre of the plant. Eventually the stalks may succumb and sag. The leaves may exhibit green-yellow blotches that eventually become ringed with red margins. Then the whole leaves will start to turn bright red, and they may wilt.

It can take two or more seasons for rhubarb plants to be completely destroyed by red leaf disease, so if you see those early warning signs, remove the infected leaves and bag them up for the landfill. Do not compost them. If you don't notice the problem until the bacteria have completely taken hold, it will unfortunately be necessary to dig up and remove the whole plant.

Aphids help spread the bacteria along by merrily feeding on infected plant parts, so controlling these little nasties if you see them is important, as well.

One final thing to note: rhubarb leaves will naturally turn red in cold weather, so don't panic unless you see evidence of all the other factors I have mentioned. If it is mid-summer, blazing hot, and the leaves are starting to show spots and colour in the wrong way, then it's time to make a diagnosis.[9] —SN

This isn't some interesting cultivar of rhubarb, unfortunately. If your rhubarb leaves start to look like this in the middle of the summer, it could be red leaf disease.

My clematis suddenly wilted and turned black. What happened?

It's early summer, and your clematis is budding out. Then suddenly, overnight it seems, it starts to wilt. Within a few days leaves and stems turn black, sometimes right to the ground. What went wrong?

The culprit is *Phoma clematidina* (formerly classified as *Ascochyta clematidina*), a wind- and water-borne fungus. It invades through leaf surfaces and occasionally

To prevent fungal infections and other issues, site your clematis plants so that they are not always sitting in damp soil.

any wounds on stems, causing a collapse of the circulatory system of the plant. No point in watering—the stems simply can no longer transport water from the roots, hence the wilting and death of above-ground structures. It is specific to the *Clematis* genus, with most species vulnerable, though the smaller-blooming varieties, such as *C. alpina*, seem to be less prone to its ravages. While wiping out a season's growth and bloom, the fungus does not infect the root systems of clematis, which gives hope for next year.

This is a fungus that overwinters in surrounding soil and in plant debris. To manage and hopefully avoid a repeat next year, do cut the infected plant right to the ground and dispose of all plant matter in the garbage. Ensure that your clematis is in a spot where its stems have good air circulation and soil is not always damp. Clematis prefer soil that is a little acidic (between 5.7 and 6.4), moisture retentive but well draining. If your soil is on the alkaline side, buffer the pH by adding compost. Mulch to avoid splashback when it rains or when watering, but avoid having the mulch too close to the crown. Finally, ensure that the vines are well supported as the stems can be easily damaged.

Then cross your fingers and hope for less humid weather next year when your clematis will bloom spectacularly once more.[10] —JM

There are tiny black balls forming on my lilies. What on earth is wrong?

Fortunately, this isn't something to worry about at all! You will usually see these interesting formations on Asiatic lilies or tiger lilies. The round black knobs are aerial bulbs, usually found at leaf axils, the intersection where the leaves meet the stems. If you plant the bulbs, in about two to four years you'll get a mature flowering lily plant, a clone of its parent.

Some lilies, including the Asiatics, also produce seed pods, which, when dry, can be cracked open to reveal small black seeds. These will not result in plants that are true to their parents, but it's fun to experiment if you have the space to do so.[11] —SN

Our Perennial Hall
of Fame

6

We've created some lists of a few of our favourite perennials that are prized for specific traits, or those that will be ideal features in specific parts of your garden or in certain conditions. If we have missed a favourite of yours, it wasn't intentional!

What are the best insectary perennials for prairie gardens?

Insectary plants, especially perennials that flower, are species that attract insects into the garden. They provide shelter, food, water, and nesting sites for a variety of insects, such as beneficial bees, butterflies, hoverflies, and lacewings. An insectary plant may also attract insects such as aphids—that we deem to be pests—but in many cases those pests attract other beneficial insects that are their natural predators. Those predators are ladybird beetles, parasitic wasps, dragonflies, damselflies, and many more. To have a truly insectary garden you have to take the rough with the smooth!

Here then are just some of best insectary herbaceous perennials for our gardens, judging by the number of insects per bloom, with something for every season.

* Basket of gold (*Aurinia saxatilis*): Masses of bright yellow blooms in spring, on sprawling plants
* Blazing star (*Liatris spicata*): A late bloomer for the bees looking for a late feast of nectar
* Catmint (*Nepeta* spp.): A sprawling plant with tiny, purple, fragrant flowers that buzzes with bees and attracts butterflies by the bazillion
* Cranesbill geranium (*Geranium maculatum*): A big hit with all insect pollinators but also birds
* Culver's root (*Veronicastrum virginicum*): Another bee feast with tall spires of mauve blooms in mid-summer; plants are sizable specimens for large gardens
* Delphiniums (*Delphinium* spp.): A larval plant for butterfly species and visited by bees
* Evening primrose (*Oenothera biennis*): Those spires of clear yellow flowers are pollinated by hawk moths and bees
* Giant hyssop (*Agastache foeniculum*): A mid-summer bloomer with spikes of fragrant purple flowers that is a nectar heaven
* Hollyhock (*Alcea rosea*): It's the single flowers that bees fall for, not the doubles

* Lamb's ears (*Stachys byzantina*): Another mint but with silver-grey fuzzy leaves and spires of small pink flowers in late summer for the bees and all
* Michaelmas daisy (*Aster amellus*): Daisy-like magenta, purple, or pink flowers are almost the last of the season and important for bees, butterflies, and flies
* Penstemons (*Penstemon* spp.): All species of penstemons have tubular flowers, often in mauve, pink, or white, and a full range of pollinators visit them, including hummingbirds!
* Peonies (*Paeonia* spp.): Have co-evolved with ants, which help open the tough sepals so the petals can burst forth
* Perennial salvias (*Salvia* spp.): Those blue-purple flowers attract bees, beetles, butterflies, and even hummingbirds
* Pincushion flower (*Scabiosa caucasica*): One of my favourite perennials; the pronounced disc with multiple florets is perfect for bees of all sorts
* Purple coneflower (*Echinacea purpurea*): A late bloomer, *E. purpurea* is important for bees and birds
* Showy goldenrod (*Solidago speciosa*): Late summer bloomers that are important for butterflies, flies, beetles, and bees
* Southern globe thistle (*Echinops ritro*): A huge plant with globelike thistly mauve flowers that swarms with bees in fall
* Spotted Joe Pye weed (*Eutrochium maculatum*): Those fuzzy rose-pink blooms are visited by bees and beetles, and butterflies too; this sizable plant is perfect for a late summer splash of colour and nectar
* Stonecrops (*Sedum* spp. for the ground covers and *Hylotelephium* spp. for the upright types): All those tiny starry flowers are great magnets for insects; autumn stonecrop, with those big blooms, is great for butterflies to land on
* Tickseeds (*Coreopsis* spp.): Those open daisy-like flowers with a central disc are perfect for small-tongued insects to feed from
* Yarrow (*Achillea millefolium*): Those dense clusters of flowers, in shades of white through pinks and yellows, are great landing pads for butterflies and are visited by beetles and predatory insects
* Yuccas (*Yucca* spp.): Stiff, sword-like foliage and great stalks of fragrant off-white blooms that are pollinated by hawk moths[1] —JM

Pollinating insects prefer coneflowers with single blooms.

Blazing star provides a source of food for pollinators late in the season.

I am looking for some outstanding native plants. What are some recommended selections?

It used to be that our perennial gardens were almost exclusively the domain of introduced species, those from other biomes and geographic regions. Native species used to be considered weedy, hard to control, and not particularly beautiful, and hey, we could always see them in the wild.

Lately, the tide is turning as we seek to conserve species under threat, both plants and the organisms that depend upon them. Native species are also hardier for our challenging and changing climate. They usually require less water and have evolved to live with the pests that are native to our areas. The benefits are manifold, but there are also some challenges to consider, namely that some native species run rampant in the garden environment, while others have very specific soil and growing conditions that gardeners cannot usually replicate.

Here then are just some of the native species of the prairies that are great additions to our gardens. There is also a wide range of nativars available.

* Blanket flowers (*Gaillardia* spp.): Named for the richly yellow through red daisy-like flowers that can blanket the landscape
* Blue-eyed grass (*Sisyrinchium montanum*): Shy, tiny blue flowers held aloft on grasslike stems
* Blue flax (*Linum lewisii*): Masses of dainty blue blooms dancing on wiry stems; loves hot and dry locations
* Brown-eyed Susan (*Rudbeckia triloba*): A late summer, golden-petalled daisy with dark brown centres for the dry slopes
* Crowfoot violet (*Viola pedatifida*): A tiny blue-purple harbinger of spring that loves to grow in grassy areas
* Dotted blazing star (*Liatris punctata*): With pink-purple spikes of blooms, they are bee magnets
* Early blue violet (*Viola adunca*): Similar to the crowfoot violet but more of a meadow and woodland denizen
* False sunflower (*Heliopsis helianthoides* var. *scabra*): Native to Saskatchewan and points east, it is also called early sunflower; bears yellow-gold, daisy-like flowers on multi-branched plants

* Fleabane (*Erigeron glabellus* var. *pubescens*): Also known as streamside or smooth fleabane; as its name suggests, it loves moist soils and even part shade; bears finely petalled pink-purple daisy-like blooms in mid-summer

* Harebell (*Campanula rotundifolia*): A dainty plant, it bears nodding, purple-blue bells on thin, wiry stems and tucks itself into crevasses and any disturbed ground that is sunny

* Marsh marigold (*Caltha palustris*): A member of the buttercup family, it bears bright yellow buttercup blooms above glossy green leaves; loves wet soils and dappled shade

* Milkweeds (*Asclepias* spp.): Known as hosts for butterflies, several species are native to the prairies; while showy milkweed (*A. speciosa*) with its fragrant, spherical pink blooms of starlike flowers is known to be the host for the monarch butterfly, the common milkweed (*A. syriaca*), swamp milkweed (*A. incarnata*), and butterfly milkweed (*A. tuberosa*) all attract a range of butterfly species

* Mountain shooting star (*Primula conjugens*): A tiny plant with purple petals folding back from the yellow centre, resembling a rocket heading for the stars; suitable for all light conditions except full shade

* Narrow-leaved coneflower (*Echinacea angustifolia*): Native to Saskatchewan and further east, this wildflower species has been hugely hybridized lately; species bears magenta-pink ray petals around a central orange-brown disc, on sturdy stems above low-growing foliage

We have a soft spot in our hearts for this diminutive beauty, commonly called prairie smoke.

Yes, it reseeds freely if you don't deadhead the flowers, but the feathery stems and brilliant blooms of blue flax are perfect additions to the native plant garden.

✳ Ostrich fern (*Matteuccia struthiopteris*) and other native ferns: Love shady and moist areas with higher humidity; while ostrich fern is common, look for others such as marginal wood fern (*Dryopteris marginalis*)

✳ Pearly everlasting (*Anaphalis margaritacea*): Long-lasting, button-small, white, daisy-like flowers held in bunches on sturdy stalks; a great substitute for milkweeds

✳ Prairie crocus (*Pulsatilla nuttalliana*): So named because it resembles a very large purple-pink crocus; hugely adaptable, it can handle part shade to full sun, and lean soils; loves to self-sow, but hates being transplanted

✳ Prairie smoke (*Geum triflorum*): Also known as old man's whiskers or three-flowered avens, this diminutive plant has three dusky-pink, nodding flowers that, as seed heads, look like giant puffballs

✳ Silvery lupine (*Lupinus argenteus*): Silvery-green palmate foliage with iconic purple-blue blooms; is most effective in drifts in full sun to part shade and likes dryish soils

✳ Star-flowered false Solomon's seal (*Maianthemum stellatum*): Strap-like foliage with graceful, starry white flowers in spring that become purple berries by fall; great for part shady areas and does best in moist soils; note it's rhizomatic, so it will spread

✳ Tall bluebells (*Mertensia paniculata*): A delicate, shy bluebell for the woodland garden; prefers moist soil and dappled light

✳ Turtlehead (*Chelone glabra*): Blooms at the end of summer with the turtle-like pink blooms that give it its common name

✳ Wild bergamot (*Monarda fistulosa*): Shaggy pink blooms top the stalks of this clumping plant; distinctive bee balm fragrance

✳ Wild columbine (*Aquilegia canadensis*): Distinctive yellow and red, downward-drooping flowers on a smaller plant than many cultivated varieties; delightfully self-sows

✳ Wild ginger (*Asarum canadense*): Heart-shaped, almost round, glossy green leaves; a great ground cover for shady gardens with deep organic soil[2] —JM

What are some perennials that are tops for foliage colour other than green?

Sometimes we like to see a different colour or two to offset all the green foliage in our gardens: purple, yellow, and chartreuse, not to mention variegated green with silver, yellow, or white. They all provide a beautiful foil or accent for the garden bed.

Here are some stunners to include in any perennial garden bed.

* Artemisias (*Artemisia* spp.): Known for their silvery foliage; 'Silvermound' is the most popular as it stays in one place but consider 'Silver Brocade' with its larger leaves or common wormwood (*A. absinthium*), which gives us the liqueur absinthe
* Astilbes (*Astilbe* spp.): Known for their plumes of white, cream, pink, or red blooms, but look for cultivars with bronze foliage or perhaps a variegated variety
* Beardtongues (*Penstemon* spp.): Have mostly green foliage but look for 'Husker Red' with red stems and red-purple foliage

This glorious bed is filled with several different types of hostas.

* Brunnera or Siberian bugloss (*Brunnera macrophylla*): Also called great forget-me-not for their tiny sky-blue flowers in spring, but it is their heart-shaped leaves, often variegated, that are desired; look for 'Jack Frost', 'Dawson's White', and 'Hadspen Cream' just to get you started

* Bugbanes (*Actaea racemosa* and *A. simplex*): Deep purple or bronzy green compound leaves are fantastic for the shady garden, along with spikes of lacy white or pink flowers late in summer

* Bugleweed (*Ajuga reptans*): Glossy burgundy and olive-green foliage; some varieties are variegated

* Coral bells (*Heuchera* spp.): Evergreen, with deeply lobed foliage with a ton of cultivars in every colour from deepest darkest purple to chartreuse, and all points in between

* Euphorbias (*Euphorbia* spp.): Known for brilliant chartreuse, red, to purple foliage and bracts; 'Fireglow', 'Candy', and 'Emerald Jade' are just a few of the many cultivars available

* False lamium or yellow archangel (*Lamium galeobdolon* 'Hermann's Pride'): Variegated silver and green foliage with sweet yellow flowers in mid-summer

When you're smitten with heucheras (which is a given, once you see them), you'll want to collect all of them for their stunning foliage. Just be sure to select varieties that can grow in your hardiness zone.

* Foamy bells (× *Heucherella*): A cross between *Heuchera* and *Tiarella*, they have deeply lobed, multicoloured foliage; perfect for light shade
* Golden Japanese spikenard (*Aralia cordata* 'Sun King'): Golden leaves in part sun to chartreuse green in fuller shade with tiny white flowers that mature deep purple (edible) berries
* Hostas (*Hosta* spp.): Big, wide, succulent foliage in hues from blue, almost yellow, cream, white, and darkest green, along with a ton of variegated cultivars; super to bring light to a shady garden
* Lamb's ears (*Stachys byzantina*): Woolly, soft, silver-grey foliage that is wonderfully tactile; you can use the leaves as a bandage if you cut yourself in the garden!
* Lungworts (*Pulmonaria* spp.): Marvellous spotted, broad leaves, and pink to blue bells in spring; so many cultivars to choose from
* Snow-in-summer (*Cerastium tomentosum*): Besides the white flowers it is the fuzzy, silver-grey foliage that makes this ground cover spectacular in a dry spot
* Stonecrops (*Sedum* spp. and *Hylotelephium* spp.): There are so many cultivars with gorgeous foliage from deep purple 'Matrona' through to 'Angelina' and 'Dragon's Blood'
* Summer phlox (*Phlox paniculata*): Look for variegated cultivars with either silver-white or cream edges. Lovely![3]

—JM

What are your recommendations for perennials for rock gardens?

Rock gardens are usually designed to take advantage of a natural rock formation in the landscape or to create the effect using rocks, stones, and pebbles. The perennials found in natural mountainous or rocky terrain generally are lower growing, due to adverse growing conditions including a short growing season, lack of rain, and wind. They have long roots designed to access available moisture and require extremely well-draining and often lean soils. Most favour at least a few hours of direct sun.

There are a diverse number of perennials that are suited for rock gardens, including some that are true alpine species. The goal for any rock garden is to emphasize the formation, particular stones, and plants that are growing in among the rocks. A tall order but beautiful when done well!

* Alpine aster (*Aster alpinus*): Pink or blue daisy flowers on this early bloomer
* Alpine cinquefoil (*Potentilla neumanniana* 'Nana'): Bright yellow flowers and evergreen foliage
* Alpine rock jasmine (*Androsace chamaejasme*): Sweet-smelling white flowers on this diminutive species, with bright orange foliage in fall
* Alpine rock thyme (*Acinos alpinus*): Tiny green leaves with magenta-pink to purple flowers held aloft
* Alumroots (*Heuchera* spp.): These aren't the fancy big-leaved ones, but shy ones for the rockery; look for *H. richardsonii* with purplish flowers or *H. parviflora* with yellow-green blooms
* Bellflowers (*Campanula* spp.): Several species work well in rock gardens; look for *C. saxifraga*, *C. turczaninowii*, or *C. topaliana* for a neat habit of growth, all with the typical bells of this genus
* Creeping baby's breath (*Gypsophila repens*): Low mats of silvery green leaves and masses of white flowers; this species is not on the invasive species lists
* Drabas (*Draba* spp.): Not drab at all! Yellow or white flowers held atop hairy, tufted basal leaves

The breathtaking colour of gentian flowers makes the low-growing varieties winners in rock gardens.

The design and structure of the flowers of hens and chicks are fascinating!

* Dragonheads (*Dracocephalum* spp.): Lance-shaped leaves with purple-blue tubular flowers
* Dwarf hairy beardtongue (*Penstemon hirsutus* var. *pygmaeus*): Mat-like mounds with, you guessed it, hairy foliage and lilac-coloured flowers
* Edelweiss (*Leontopodium alpinum*): Lance-shaped, woolly foliage and white, star-shaped, tiny flowers
* Fleabanes (*Erigeron* spp.): Look for smaller varieties such as *E. montanensis* or *E. scopulinus* for ground-hugging foliage and outsize, finely cut, daisy-like flowers
* Gentians, trumpet gentian (*Gentiana verna*): With those true-blue outsize blooms above a low carpet of green leaves; there are other low-growing gentians to pursue too
* Harebell (*Campanula alaskana*): Blue-purple bells held on wiry slender stems
* Hens and chicks (*Sempervivum tectorum*): Flat to the ground, succulent rosettes

* Iceland poppies (*Papaver nudicaule*): Orange or yellow flowers on wiry stems throughout summer
* Mossy saxifrage (*Saxifraga × arendsii*): Pincushion mounds with delicate rose flowers, prefers partial shade
* Pheasant's eye (*Adonis vernalis*): Big yellow blooms above ferny foliage in spring
* Red creeping thyme (*Thymus praecox*): Carpets of rose-pink flowers that spread slowly
* Rock cress (*Aubrieta deltoidea*): Little purple flowers early in spring, and dainty foliage
* Rock or sun rose (*Helianthemum nummularium*): A shrubby, evergreen perennial covered in roselike flowers in a rainbow of colours
* Stonecrops (*Sedum* spp. and *Hylotelephium* spp.): Lots and lots of variety; one of my favourites for the rockery is *S. lanceolatum* with its starry yellow flowers
* Thrift (*Armeria maritima*): Neat little evergreen clumps with lavender to rose-pink flowers[4] —JM

I need some useful ground cover perennials. What would you suggest?

Ground cover herbaceous perennials are true multi-functional plants. Hugging the ground with foliage only an inch (2.5 centimetres) or so tall, they are beautiful, covered when in bloom with masses of tiny flowers. As a group, they serve as a living mulch protecting the soil and roots of other plants. Ground covers of all sorts prevent soil erosion as well as compaction from heavy rains and even foot traffic, and they harbour insects of all kinds. From a design perspective, they provide another layer of interest and blooming time in the garden. Finally, they can be truly low-maintenance perennials, gently creeping and spreading over and into every nook and cranny. Here are a few that may fit the bill in your garden.

* Bugleweed or carpet bugle (*Ajuga reptans*): Glossy dark green or burgundy leaves along with three-inch (eight-centimetre) dainty violet flower spikes in spring; this one will take over your grass if you let it—I don't have grass
* Candytuft (*Iberis sempervirens*): I bought one years ago and have transplanted it all over my garden; a beautiful, evergreen, prostrate ground cover with starry white flowers mid-spring
* Creeping or moss phlox (*Phlox subulata*): Great for hot and dry areas with evergreen, rosemary-like foliage and tons of pink or mauve flowers in late spring
* Dwarf speedwell (*Veronica pectinata*): Dense mats of grey-green leaves and blue or rose flowers in July
* European ginger (*Asarum europaeum*): Fabulous for deep shade; thick, glossy, rounded, dark green leaves are its main feature; mine grows inside the drip line of my spruce
* Fairy's thimble (*Campanula cochlearifolia*): A terrific dwarf bellflower, with tiny blue bells held over delicate rounded leaves; it is rhizomatous, but not aggressive
* Golden creeping Jenny (*Lysimachia nummularia*): This one I grow so I can divide it ruthlessly and use it in my annual containers; a bit too aggressive for my taste on the whole, but lovely in shady areas

Fragrant and pretty, sweet woodruff is an ideal ground cover selection for shaded spots.

✳ Hens and chicks (*Sempervivum tectorum*): Dense, evergreen, succulent rosettes that are super anchors in dry and hot locations; you don't have to do anything, just let them go and grow

✳ Lily of the valley (*Convallaria majalis*): Despite its reputation, this one with its sweet-smelling, tulip-like foliage will fill difficult areas like nothing else, and be welcome — make sure it is strictly contained, and you will love it

✳ Maiden pink (*Dianthus deltoides*): Cushions of narrow needle-like leaves covered in mid-summer with fringed flowers in shades of red, pink, and white; loves sun

✳ Periwinkle (*Vinca minor*): An evergreen, vining ground cover with glossy, dark green leaves and purple or white flowers; where the nodes touch the soil, it will anchor there, so a great one for the shady hillside

✳ Pussytoes (*Antennaria rosea*): Absolutely flat to the ground with grey-green leaves, these are a must for dry, hot, exposed areas; the pink rosette flowers, held aloft on wiry stems, look for all the world like the pad of a kitten's paw

✳ Rock cress (*Arabis alpina* or *A. alpina* subsp. *caucasica*): Soft greyish foliage with tons of tiny white flowers (occasionally pink) that dance above in May; loves lots of sun and well-draining soil

✳ Rock soapwort (*Saponaria ocymoides*): Careful with this one—I have mine under my spruce so it doesn't go crazy; the bright pink flowers brighten up the space in mid-summer

✳ Saxifrages (*Saxifraga* spp.): Lots of different species for our gardens, with mossy saxifrage (*S. bryoides*) the better known; my fave is encrusted saxifrage (*S. paniculata*), which is tough as nails yet sends out thin stalks with panicles of starry white flowers in June

✳ Stemless gentian (*Gentiana acaulis*): Spectacular and coveted with outsize true-blue trumpets that spring from glossy, deep green leaves; prefers moister soils and partial shade but can handle sun

✳ Stonecrops (*Sedum* spp. and *Hylotelephium* spp.): So many choices; with their succulent leaves and starry flowers come summer, they spread where you let them but are easy to control; definitely full sun and dry soils for these

✳ Sweet woodruff (*Galium odoratum*): Palmate leaves and white sweet-smelling flowers; loves the shade but can handle full sun

✳ Thymes (*Thymus* spp.): Whether it is creeping thyme (*T. serpyllum*) or woolly thyme (*T. pseudolanuginosus*), these dense, aromatic mats covered with purple or pink flowers are a staple[5]

PS. Anyone who has heard me rant about dead nettle (*Lamium maculatum*) knows that this is one that I positively love to hate. I yank it out by the handfuls. Once it's in the garden bed, try getting it out!—JM

What are some appealingly fragrant perennials?

Scent in the garden can be a highly attractive trait. Plant these lovelies where your sniffer can best discover them!

* Bearded iris (*Iris germanica*): The downward petals (called falls) on the flowers are fuzzy, hence the reference to a beard in the common name; a sun lover
* Garden phlox (*Phlox paniculata*): Stunningly showy flower heads and strong fragrance
* Gas plant (*Dictamnus alba*): Lovely lemony fragrance
* Sweet iris (*Iris pallida* 'Variegata'): Smells like grape Kool-Aid!
* Sweet william (*Dianthus barbatus*): An old-fashioned cottage garden favourite; looks stellar in drifts

Other selections we've already mentioned, such as bee balm (*Monarda* spp.), lily of the valley (*Convallaria majalis*), and sweet woodruff (*Galium odoratum*) are also beautifully fragrant.[6]—SN & JM

Gas plant has it all: brawn, beauty, and a delightful fragrance!

You can clearly see how much certain pollinators adore bee balm, but its gorgeous fragrance is another big reason to give it a place in your garden.

What are the best of the big and bold perennials?

If you need eye-popping focal points for your garden, plants that aren't ashamed to draw attention with their beauty and seriously big bones, look no further than these massive specimens.

* Delphiniums (*Delphinium* spp.): The giant varieties will need staking, but those gorgeous racemes are worth it!
* False sunflower (*Heliopsis helianthoides*): Also called rough heliopsis due to the texture of the leaves; the yellow daisy-like flowers are borne in masses and the plants look great in drifts
* Giant meadow rue (*Thalictrum rochebrunianum*): Striking foliage that looks like that of a columbine; deer *sometimes* leave it alone
* Goat's beard (*Aruncus dioicus*): Feathery leaves and panicles of frothy flowers make this giant perennial a standout
* Leopard plant (*Ligularia przewalskii*): Shade lover, prefers soil with even moisture
* Monkshood (*Aconitum napellus*): Another shade lover; lipped blooms are found on tall spikes
* Sneezeweed (*Helenium autumnale*): Gorgeous in cut flower arrangements, excellent planted in drifts[7] —SN

Leopard plant is a bold statement plant for that shady spot in your garden.

I am looking for effective drought-tolerant perennials. What are some great picks?

Prolonged periods of dry weather are common on the prairies. At the same time, more gardeners are seeking ways to minimize water use in their garden. One of the most important keys to dealing with both sides of that coin is plant selection. Try these drought-tolerant perennials in your water-wise garden.

* Alliums (*Allium* spp.): So many gorgeous ornamental alliums to choose from; instantly recognizable for their fuzzy round flowers

* Bee balms (*Monarda didyma* and *M. fistulosa*): Bee balm has it all: fragrance, good looks, drought tolerance, and it's an amazing pollinator plant, to boot

* Blanket flowers (*Gaillardia* spp.): A low-maintenance, sun-loving perennial with bold, colourful blooms

* Blazing stars (*Liatris* spp.): With attractive, fuzzy-looking floral stalks; a great selection for sunny spots

* Catmints (*Nepeta* × *faassenii* and *N. mussinii*): As befitting members of the mint family, these guys are rather easy to please and tolerate dry soils very well

Alliums are excellent choices for dry gardens.

* Dianthus (*Dianthus* spp.): Versatile, with many species and growth habits
* Lungworts (*Pulmonaria* spp.): Gorgeous spotted foliage and beautiful tubular flowers in early spring
* Prairie smoke (*Geum triflorum*): A true prairie grassland denizen
* Russian sage (*Salvia yangii*): This large, fragrant perennial fits many bills, including loving sunny sites and putting up with a lack of H_2O
* Southern globe thistle (*Echinops ritro*): Eye-catching flowers are excellent for cutting; not a true thistle
* Speedwells (*Veronica spicata* and *V. longifolia*): Spiked flowers are highly desired by bees
* Stonecrops (*Sedum* spp. or *Hylotelephium* spp.): A wide range of varieties and colours to choose from — SN

Whether in flower or seed, globe thistles have some of the most interesting features in the garden.

What are the top perennial selections for shade?

If you have a spot in your garden that isn't bright with sunshine, don't despair— these plants don't need a ton of light to thrive. Part shade (about four hours of sunlight a day) is sufficient.

✳ Astilbes (*Astilbe* spp.): Available in several flower colours; the frothy blooms are borne on tall stalks

✳ Bleeding heart (*Lamprocapnos spectabilis*): Dainty, dangling flowers and spectacular foliage, goes dormant in the heat of summer

✳ Brunnera (*Brunnera macrophylla*): Stunning foliage and delicate flowers

✳ Bugbane (*Actaea simplex*): Prefers consistently damp soils in woodland-style gardens; gorgeous foliage and small but appealing flowers

✳ Bugleweed (*Ajuga reptans*): A low, spreading ground cover with highly attractive leaves

✳ Goat's beard (*Aruncus dioicus*): Sizable perennial with creamy feathery flowers

✳ Hostas (*Hosta* spp.): With countless varieties it's easy to want to collect hostas for their incredible foliage

✳ Toad lily (*Tricyrtis formosana*): Brilliant spotted flowers are a standout in the shade garden[8]—SN

118

Which perennials are happiest in a sunny location?

Does your garden receive six or more hours of full sun each day? These selections are perfect candidates for your site.

* Avens (*Geum* spp.): There are several types of plants to choose from in this attractive genus, with differing appearances
* Beardtongues (*Penstemon* spp.): Several hardy types for the prairies, definitely statement plants with their tall floral stalks
* Candytuft (*Iberis sempervirens*): Beautiful mounding growth habit and masses of small white blooms; some cultivars have purple or pink flowers
* Cranesbills (*Geranium* spp.): Don't mix this up with the annual pelargonium; this hardy perennial is very low maintenance
* Creeping thyme (*Thymus serpyllum*): Delectable fragrance on low-growing spreading plants, perfect for planting between stepping stones

Painted daisies are positively showstopping when planted in large groups.

* Day lilies (*Hemerocallis* spp.): Various plant sizes and bloom colours make this another plant that is easy to collect
* Lamb's ears (*Stachys byzantina*): The texture of the foliage is adorable; the flowers are surprising and unusual on fuzzy stalks; will bloom late into the season
* Maiden pink (*Dianthus deltoides*): Traditional cottage favourite with pretty frilly flowers, best planted in masses
* Painted daisy (*Tanacetum coccineum*): Cheerful, colourful blooms look to be straight out of a crayon box
* Peonies (*Paeonia* spp.): Diverse range of floral forms and colours and attractive foliage on long-lived plants—what's not to love?
* Thrift (*Armeria maritima*): Watch the water on this diminutive beauty with grasslike foliage; does best in dry soil
* Wood asters (*Eurybia* spp., formerly included in *Aster* spp.): Many species and cultivars of this reliable, adaptable, daisy-like perennial available
* Woolly thyme (*Thymus pseudolanuginosus*): Cute, fuzzy, fragrant ground cover[9] —SN

I am eager to have some spring colour! What are some early-blooming perennials?

Surely one of the best reasons to grow perennials is that they are often the ones that come up first, with fresh, bright green foliage and the promise of beautiful things to come.

And the bees and other pollinators love them dearly.

I couldn't greet spring without that earliest of all, liverleaf (*Hepatica nobilis*), with its shy mauve-blue blooms out even before the new leaves or mounds of our native prairie crocus (*Pulsatilla nuttalliana*) with their nodding heads on south-facing slopes.

Here then is a selection for consideration for inclusion in your garden that typically bloom from April through late May depending on your location and the weather of course.

* Basket of gold (*Aurinia saxatilis*): The name says it all
* Bergenia (*Bergenia cordifolia*): Broadleaf evergreen with stalks of pink flowers
* Bleeding heart (*Lamprocapnos spectabilis*): Such an old-fashioned favourite
* Bloodroot (*Sanguinaria canadensis*): Pure white flowers in spring—don't blink or you will miss them, but a real treasure; the name refers to the fact that the sap in the root is blood red
* Bluebells (*Mertensia virginica* and *M. paniculata*): Nothing says spring like bluebells!
* Hellebores (*Helleborus* spp.): The Christmas rose, if we didn't happen to have winter like we do
* Leopard's bane (*Doronicum caucasicum*): To be different, this one is a bright yellow daisy
* Lungworts (*Pulmonaria* spp.): So named for its spotted leaves, just like a lung, but comes with dainty pink flowers that turn sky blue; so many different cultivars to choose for different leaves

It's difficult not to get a little misty-eyed with joy when you see the magnificent flowers of Hepatica after a bitterly long winter.

✳ Marsh marigold (*Caltha palustris*): A plant for a really moist location; buttercup-yellow flowers

✳ Prairie crocus (*Pulsatilla nuttalliana*): A true harbinger of spring; also known as pasque flower as it often is in bloom around Easter

✳ Primroses (*Primula* spp.): I love them all, whether it's the soft yellow of oxlip (*P. elatior*) or brasher yellow of cowslip (*P. veris*), or the leathery-leaved auricula primrose (*P. auricula*) with clusters of yellow, mauve, purple, and cream flowers around a yellow centre; there are others too, the taller mauve drumstick primrose (*P. denticulata*) and of course the English primrose (*P. vulgaris*) you bought last year at a grocery store to brighten your winter and planted in the garden

✳ Rock cress (*Aubrieta deltoidea*): Mats of dense cross-shaped flowers in purple or mauve

Hellebores are another exquisite and extremely early-blooming spring perennial.

* Shooting star (*Primula meadia* syn. *Dodecatheon meadia*): A lovely species, with rose-pink or white miniature rocket-shaped flowers held on thin upright stalks
* Snowdrop anemone (*Anemone sylvestris*): Swaths of nodding white flowers
* Wild blue phlox (*Phlox divaricata*): Carpets of blue flowers[10]

—JM

I want all-season coverage in my garden! What are some late-blooming perennials that will bloom in late summer or early autumn?

One of the keys to a perennial garden that keeps blooming throughout the whole growing season is careful plant selection. You need to consider not only the early and mid-season bloomers in the garden, but the late ones as well. Here are some of the latter to help you plan a perennial garden with colour that lasts!

＊ Balloon flower (*Platycodon grandiflorus*): Striking puffy blooms are borne on slender stalks

＊ Black-eyed Susans (*Rudbeckia* spp.): Sun-loving, bold flowers perfect for drift planting

＊ False sunflower (*Heliopsis helianthoides*): Cheerful blooms that resemble miniature sunflowers

＊ Giant hyssop (*Agastache foeniculum*): Attractive tall flower stalks and a delightful licorice scent

＊ Pearly everlasting (*Anaphalis margaritacea*): Long-lasting, button-small, white, daisy-like flowers held in bunches on sturdy stalks

＊ Showy aster (*Eurybia conspicua*): A wonderful type for the late-season garden with its large blooms

＊ Sneezeweed (*Helenium autumnale*): Brilliant colour spices up the late summer garden and takes it into autumn

＊ Stonecrops (*Sedum* spp. and *Hylotelephium* spp.): Look for varieties such as 'Autumn Joy' and 'Matrona'

＊ Tickseeds (*Coreopsis* spp.): Gorgeous flowers are seriously bee friendly; showstopping when planted in masses[11] —SN

I need a fast-growing perennial climbing vine for my garden. Do you have any recommendations?

If there is anything that is truly a challenge on the prairies it has to be a fast-growing perennial herbaceous vine! Here are a few woody vines that thrive on the prairies, incrementally extending their reach each year as their vines thicken and twist around their supports and we joyously embrace them.

* Clematis (*Clematis* spp.): These beauties are classified into groups A, B, and C, according to whether they bloom on old or new wood (group A are woody, while groups B and C are treated as herbaceous perennials); most clematis grow six to nine feet (two to three metres) each year; look for Jackman's clematis (C. × 'Jackmanii'), the most dependable of the bunch for the prairies, as well as 'Ernest Markham', 'Rouge Cardinal', 'Comtesse de Bouchard', and 'Polish Spirit'
* Hops (*Humulus lupulus*) and golden hops (*H. lupulus* 'Aureus'): Grows up to twenty feet (seven metres) each growing season; cut back to the crown after the top growth has died away; attractive heart-shaped leaves and interesting fruit in autumn
* Sweet autumn clematis (*Clematis terniflora*): Native to Asia, masses of tiny, fragrant flowers in late summer; be careful of this one—it grows exponentially and can take over anything it grows in or on[12]—JM

Sweet autumn clematis has beautiful creamy flowers and it will cover a trellis or other support in no time!

Hops require strong supports due to their vigorous, speedy growth.

What are some perennials to be careful about due to their toxicity?

Plants have developed a wide range of toxins as a means of defence from predators. These chemicals include nicotine, caffeine, solanine, digitalis, aconitine, and piperidine. Many plants have only one part that is toxic, with the rest edible. Others are toxic from top to bottom. The toxins plants contain can be poisonous if ingested, and some are a danger if brushed up against or even if their sap gets on our skin. Most will not kill us but will cause significant distress if consumed. Some are fine for people but affect our cats and dogs. Others are terrible for horses and cows. Many would require you to eat bushels of their foliage to have an ill effect yet are feared. Others require just unwary handling to be dangerous.

Monkshood is gorgeous but not to be trifled with!

Although it behooves us to learn which of our favourite plants could be a danger to people, pets, and wildlife, it does not mean that we need to necessarily ban them from our gardens. Planted in the right location, either away from curious fingers or protected from easy access, they can still be a part of the garden. Educating ourselves and those who visit our gardens is a big part of ensuring we are safe. Learning respect for those plants is vital too, just as we learn to respect the more obvious physical danger from thorns and prickles.

Here are some of the common perennials we include in our gardens that demand our respect.

* Bleeding heart (*Lamprocapnos spectabilis*): All parts
* Coneflowers (*Rudbeckia* spp.): All parts
* Delphinium (*Delphinium* spp.): All parts
* Fleabane (*Erigeron* spp.): All parts
* Foxglove (*Digitalis purpurea*): All parts, very toxic
* Hellebore (*Helleborus* spp.): Everything except the flowers
* Iris (*Iris* spp.): Leaves and rhizomes
* Lily of the valley (*Convallaria majalis*): All parts
* Lobelia (*Lobelia* spp.): Leaves and seeds
* Monkshood (*Aconitum* spp.): All parts, very toxic
* Poppies (*Papaver* spp.): Everything except for ripe seeds
* Rhubarb (*Rheum rhabarbarum*): Leaves[13] —JM

Trees and shrubs are the bones of the garden, but it is herbaceous perennials that clothe the garden with infinite variations of form, foliage, and colourful blooms. While annuals come and go, it is our perennials that are always there, steadfast and true. We hope they delight your senses (and your green thumbs) as much as they do ours!

Acknowledgements

From Janet and Sheryl:

We can't adequately express how much the support, encouragement, commitment, and dedication of the entire publishing team at TouchWood Editions continues to mean to us! Thank you all from the bottom of our hearts: Tori Elliott (publisher), Kate Kennedy (editorial coordinator), Curtis Samuel (publicist and social media coordinator), Warren Layberry (copy editor), Meg Yamamoto (proofreader), Sydney Barnes (typesetter), and Pat Touchie (owner). A very special thank you goes out to designer Tree Abraham. We are also incredibly appreciative of the support and encouragement of Taryn Boyd. Without her, we would have never embarked on this journey. We cannot thank her enough for everything she has done for us!

Many thanks to Andy Schalk, who generously contributed a photo to the book.

We would like to mention how immensely grateful we are to our readers, who have been so enthusiastic about the books and exponentially increased our ratio of warm fuzzies.

From Janet:

It was my English mother who introduced me to perennials and started my love affair with them. Long gone, my gardening mum still resonates in my garden through the plants that honour her. I bless her every time I am in my garden.

As always, I am profoundly thankful for my long-suffering family, who help me care for the garden be it with watering, lugging plants and soil, or living with the garden that refuses to stay outside.

From Sheryl:

Heaps of love to Rob, Mum and Dad, and Derek. And a huge thank you to all of my friends at the Calgary Public Library for their support. I am so fortunate to work with such absolutely incredible people.

Notes

Introduction

1. Shakespeare, *Romeo and Juliet*, in *The Globe Illustrated Shakespeare*, 174.

2. Cambridge Dictionary (website), "Perennial."

3. Biology Dictionary (website), "Herbaceous."

4. Shinn, "Forbs: What Is a Forb?," *Horticulture* (website); Beaulieu, "What Are Herbaceous Plants?," The Spruce (website); Capon, *Botany for Gardeners*, 3rd ed., 62–64.

5. Capon, *Botany for Gardeners*, 3rd ed., 16, 221.

6. Badgett, "Sempervivum Is Dying: Fixing Drying Leaves on Hens and Chicks," Gardening Know How (website); Greenshack (website), "Can Plants Live Forever? (Detailed Explanation)."

Chapter One

1. National Gardening Association (website), "Terminology: Genus and Species."

2. Haynes, "Cultivar versus Variety," Iowa State University Extension and Outreach (website); Martin, "Native Species or Cultivars of Native Plants," Piedmont Master Gardeners (website); Tangren, "Cultivars of Native Plants," University of Maryland Extension (website).

3. Martin, "Native Species or Cultivars of Native Plants," Piedmont Master Gardeners (website).

4. Schmidt, "Coneflowers: Native vs Hybrid," Dyck Arboretum (website).

5. Martin, "Native Species or Cultivars of Native Plants," Piedmont Master Gardeners (website); Tangren, "Cultivars of Native Plants," University of Maryland Extension (website); Lorecentral (website), "Advantages and Disadvantages of Hybridization in Plants"; Pearman and Pike, *NatureScape Alberta*, 22–23.

6. Garland, "Native versus Non-native: Which Plants Are Best for Biodiversity?," The Nature of Cities (website).

7. Hettinger, "Conceptualizing and Evaluating Non-native Species," The Nature Knowledge Education Project (website).

8. Dunnett, *Naturalistic Planting Design*, 72–74.

9. Pearman and Pike, *NatureScape Alberta*, 17–18, 28–33.

10. Rainer and West, *Planting in a Post-Wild World*, 20–23; Espace pour la vie (website), "Native, Exotic, Naturalized or Invasive"; Lewis, "Where the Wild Things Are: How to Support Wildlife in the Modern Gardening World," Ecological Landscape Alliance (website).

11. Rainer and West, *Planting in a Post-Wild World*, 80–89, 176–84; Pearman and Pike, *NatureScape Alberta*, 17–18, 28–33; Riordan and Robinson, "Top Tips for a Biodiverse Garden," Royal Botanic Gardens Kew (website); Espace pour la vie (website), "Gardening for Biodiversity"; University of Saskatchewan (website), "Creating Biodiversity in Your Yard."

12. Paraspace (website), "Plant Hardiness Zones in Canada: How Do They Work?"; Government of Canada (website), "Plant Hardiness Zones."

13. Rainer and West, *Planting in a Post-Wild World*, 43–47; Toop and Williams, *Perennials for the Prairies*, 28; Siegel, "Design Theory: How Many Plants Do You Need?," *Fine Gardening* (website).

Chapter Two

1. de Long, "Dividing Perennials," Cornell Cooperative Extension (website); Bloomin Designs Nursery (website), "The Root of the Perennial Plant"; *Post Bulletin* (website), "Growing Concerns: Root Systems Have a Role to Play in Plant Division"; Oregon State University (website), "Perennials: How to Dig and Divide!"

2. Laidback Gardener (website), "Head in the Sun, Feet in the Shade."

3. Toop and Williams, *Perennials for the Prairies*, 17–18; Dawson and Peters, *Perennials for Alberta*, 20–21; Toronto Master Gardeners (website), "Determining Sun Quality"; Regina Gardening Associates Inc. (website), "Perennial Flowers for Partial Sun to Full Sun"; Proven Winners (website), "What Does Full Sun or Part Shade Mean?"

4. Science and Plants for Schools (website), "Some Physical Differences between Sun and Shade Plants."

5. Walliser, "Shade-Loving Perennial Flowers: 15 Beautiful Choices," Savvy Gardening (website); Barber, "Characteristics of Shade Plants," SFGATE (website).

6. Toop and Williams, *Perennials for the Prairies*, 13–15.

7. Walters Gardens (website), "The Complete Guide to Growing Perennials in Containers"; Belgian Nursery (website), "Growing Perennials in Pots and Planters."

Chapter Three

1. DeJohn, "Grow Perennials from Seed," Gardener's Supply Company (website); Salisbury Greenhouse (website), "How to Grow Your Favourite Perennials from Seed."

2. Wildfong, "Stratification for Dormant Seeds," Seeds of Diversity (website); Restoration Seeds (website), "Germinating Perennial Seeds"; Patterson, "Seed Stratification: What Seeds Require Cold Treatment," Gardening Know How (website).

3. M. Smith, *The Plant Propagator's Bible*, 170.

4. J. Rhoades, "False Indigo Growing Tips: Growing and Caring for Baptisia Plants," Gardening Know How (website).

5. Johnstone, "How to Grow Gas Plants," The Spruce (website).

6. Salisbury Greenhouse (website), "How to Grow Your Favourite Perennials from Seed"; DeJohn, "Grow Perennials from Seed," Gardener's Supply Company (website); Kelaidis, "10 Perennials Easily Grown from Seed," *Fine Gardening* (website); *Garden Gate* (website), "Perennial Seeds to Plant in Fall"; Ianotti, "10 Perennial Flowers to Start from Seed," The Spruce (website); Will, "25 Annual and Perennial Flower Seeds to Sow in Fall," Empress of Dirt (website).

7. Lima, *The Perennial Garden*, 144–46; Weisenhorn and Furgeson, "How and When to Divide Perennials," University of Minnesota Extension (website); Forney, "When to Divide Perennials," HGTV (website).

8. Lima, *The Perennial Garden*, 144–46; Dawson and Peters, *Perennials for Alberta*, 56–57; Valleau, "Dividing Perennials in the Spring," Perennials.com;

132

Johnson, "Fall Is a Great Time to Divide Perennials, but Don't Wait Too Long," *Chicago Tribune* (website); Weisenhorn and Furgeson, "How and When to Divide Perennials," University of Minnesota Extension (website).

9. Weisenhorn and Furgeson, "How and When to Divide Perennials," University of Minnesota Extension (website); University of New Hampshire (website), "When Should I Divide My Perennials?"

10. Cook, "Dividing Peonies," Canadian Peony Society (website); Forney, "Transplanting Peonies," HGTV (website).

11. Sweetser, "How to Cut Back Perennials in Fall," *The Old Farmer's Almanac* (website); Knauss and Hubbard, "Cutting Down Perennials in the Fall," PennState Extension (website).

12. University of Illinois Extension (website), "Gardening with Perennials: After Planting Care."

13. University of Illinois Extension (website), "Gardening with Perennials: After Planting Care."

14. Beaulieu, "When to Remove Mulch from Perennials in Spring," The Spruce (website).

15. *Fine Gardening* (website), "Six Tips for Effective Weed Control"; Connors, "Weeding Made Easy: Tips and Tricks," Homesteading.com.

16. Lima, *The Perennial Garden*, 39; University of New Hampshire (website), "What Is the Best Way to Deadhead Perennials?"; Beaulieu, "Why You Should Be Deadheading Plants," The Spruce (website); Tilley, "Deadheading Flowers: Encouraging a Second Bloom in the Garden," Gardening Know How (website); *Gardens Illustrated* (website), "Best Plants for Winter Seedheads."

17. Grant, "What Is Reseeding: How to Manage Self-Seeders in Gardens," Gardening Know How (website); Myers, "Managing Self-Seeding Perennials."

18. Neveln, "Staking and Training Perennials," *Better Homes and Gardens* (website); Gardener's Supply Company, "How to Choose Flower Supports."

19. Passiglia's Nursery and Garden Center (website), "What to Do When Your Perennials Don't Come Up."

20. Weigel, "Do Perennial Flowers Need to Be Covered If There Is a Frost," PennLive.com.

21. Perennials.com, "Saving and Starting Perennials Seeds"; Hughes, "How to Save Seeds from Your Garden to Plant Next Year," *Better Homes and Gardens* (website); Allonsy, "How to Reseed Perennials," SFGATE (website); Jabbour, "Collecting Seeds from Your Garden," Savvy Gardening (website).

22. Salisbury Greenhouse (website), "How to Move Plants Indoors for Winter"; Sweetser, "How to Bring Outdoor Plants Indoors," *The Old Farmer's Almanac* (website); Plant Perfect (website), "Tender Perennials You Can Keep as Houseplants Over Winter."

Chapter Four

1. Sproule, "Growing Asparagus in Alberta," Salisbury Greenhouse (website); Calgary Gardening (website), "Planting Asparagus Crowns in Calgary."

2. H. Rhoades, "Cutting Asparagus Foliage Back in Autumn," Gardening Know How (website); Iowa State University (website), "When Can I Cut Back My Asparagus Foliage?"

3. Shaw, "The Bracken Fern: A Natural Born Killer?," *The Atlantic* (website).

4. Government of Canada (website), "Food Safety Tips for Fiddleheads."

5. Watson and Alfaro, "What Are Fiddlehead Ferns?," The Spruce Eats (website); Ostrich Ferns (website), "Ostrich Ferns."

6. Neverman, "Before You Plant Sunchokes, You Need to Read This Post," Common Sense Home (website); H. Rhoades, "Growing Horseradish: How to Grow Horseradish," Gardening Know How (website); Rayment, *The Northern Gardener*, 72–73, 129; Bradley, *The Pruner's Bible*, 210–11; Patterson, "Invasive Plant List: Learn about What Plants Are Aggressive," Gardening Know How (website); Iannotti, "10 Aggressively Spreading Plants and How to Deal with Them," The Spruce (website).

7. Stevenson, "Frost-Touched Rhubarb Can Be Poisonous," *Manitoba Co-operator* (website); Iowa State University (website), "Is It Safe to Eat Rhubarb after the Plants Have Been Exposed to Freezing Temperatures?"

8. Thomson, "What Exactly IS Rhubarb, Anyway?," HuffPost (website).

9. Lerner, "Rhubarb Flowers Blooming or Bolting?," Purdue University (website).

10. Engeland, *Growing Great Garlic*, 14, 145–46; Kelsey, *Edible Perennial Gardening*, 76; Adamant, "Growing Garlic as a Perennial," Practical Self Reliance (website).

11. Kelsey, *Edible Perennial Gardening*, 84; Wilson, "9 Beautiful Edible Ornamental Plants," Grow Network (website); Engels, "Ornamental Plants That Are Edible and/or Edible Plants That Are Ornamental," Permaculture Research Institute (website).

Chapter Five

1. Gibson, "Red Lily Beetle (*Lilioceris lilii*)," B&D Lilies (website); T. Smith, "Lily Leaf Beetle," University of Massachusetts Amherst (website); Olds College (website), "The Lily Beetle."

2. University of Saskatchewan (website), "Delphinium Worm"; Murphy, "How to Get Rid of Delphinium Worms," Gardening with Sharon (website).

3. American Daylily Society (website), "Gall Midge"; British Columbia Ministry of Agriculture (website), "Daylily Hemerocallis Gall Midge."

4. Uelmen, "Hollyhock Rust," Wisconsin Horticulture Division of Extension (website); Missouri Botanical Garden (website), "Rust of Hollyhock"; Iowa State University (website), "Hollyhock Rust"; Demers, Romberg, and Castlebury, "Microcyclic Rusts of Hollyhock (*Alcea rosea*)," National Library of Medicine (website).

5. Missouri Botanical Garden (website), "Botrytis Blight"; Carroll, "Gray Mold Control: Learn about the Treatment of Botrytis Blight," Gardening Know How (website); Michigan State University (website), "Botrytis Blight."

6. Brown, "Fact Sheet: Anthracnose Disease of Ornamental Plants: A Pictorial," University of Florida (website); Downer, Swain, and Crump, "Anthracnose," University of California (website); Planet Natural Research Center (website), "Anthracnose."

7. Spengler, "Problems with Peonies: Reasons Peony Buds Don't Develop," Gardening Know How (website); Missouri Botanical Garden (website), "Bud-Blast of Peony."

8. Hudelson and Jull, "Root and Crown Rots," Wisconsin Horticulture (website); Missouri Botanical Garden (website), "Root, Stem, Crown, and Collar Rot"; Tilley, "Crown Rot Identification and Tips for Crown Rot Treatment," Gardening Know How (website).

9. Pacific Northwest Pest Management Handbooks (website), "Rhubarb (*Rheum rhabarbarum*)—Red Leaf"; Agri-Facts (website), "Rhubarb Production in Alberta."

10. Pacific Northwest Pest Management Handbooks (website), "Clematis—Leaf and Stem Spot"; Missouri Botanical Garden (website), "Clematis Wilt."

11. Myers, "What to Do with Asiatic Lily Seed Pods"; B&D Lilies (website), "Be Mindful of Lily Bulblets."

Chapter Six

1. University of California (website), "Insectary Plants"; *Mother Earth News* (website), "Organic Pest Control: The Best Plants to Attract Beneficial Insects and Bees"; Johnny's Selected Seeds (website), "Plants for Insectaries"; Harlequin's Gardens (website), "Insectary Plants: Let Nature Manage the Pests."

2. Flanagan, *Native Plants for Prairie Gardens*, 2, 97–100, 107–8, 112–13, 115, 121, 125–28; Scholtens, "Why Grow Native Plants?," Canadian Wildlife Federation (website); Hidden Habitat Ecological Landscapes (website), "Benefits of Using Native Plants"; Prairie Originals (website), "Wildflowers for Dry to Medium Soil."

3. Dawson and Peters, *Perennials for Alberta*, 72–79, 84–87, 104–5, 120–23, 168–69, 190–95, 264–67, 303–9; Jauron, "Perennials with Colorful Foliage," Iowa State University (website); Loughrey, "Heuchera—the Ultimate Guide to Coral Bells from Proven Winners," Proven Winners (website).

4. Vale's Greenhouse, "Alpine Garden"; Landscape Ontario (website), "Perennials for Your Rock Garden"; Wild about Flowers (website), "Browse by Latin Name."

5. Toop and Williams, *Perennials for the Prairies*, 62, 65, 68, 78, 80, 86, 88, 101, 110, 116, 135, 148, 150–51, 155, 158; Dawson and Peters, *Perennials for Alberta*, 136–37, 186–87, 292–93, 302–5, 308–9; Tannas, *Common Plants*

of the Western Rangelands, vol. 3, 58, 261–64, 384; Salisbury Greenhouse (website), "8 Great Groundcovers for Zone 3 Gardens"; Walliser, "Evergreen Groundcover Plants: 20 Choices for Year-Round Interest," Savvy Gardening (website).

6. Toop and Williams, *Perennials for the Prairies*, 86, 88, 91, 112–13, 126, 128, 136.

7. Toop and Williams, *Perennials for the Prairies*, 60, 71, 87, 95, 107, 118, 153; Hole, *Perennial Favorites*, 196–97, 294–95.

8. Millcreek Nursery Ltd. (website), "Hillside Black Beauty Bugbane"; Badgett, "Toad Lily Care: Information about the Toad Lily Plant," Gardening Know How (website).

9. Mahr, "Sea Thrift, *Armeria maritima*," Wisconsin Horticulture (website); Masterclass (website), "How to Grow Candytuft Flowers: 5 Care Tips for Candytufts."

10. Toop and Williams, *Perennials for the Prairies*, 64–65, 74, 76, 91, 110, 126, 142–43, 144, 147; Hole, *Perennial Favorites*, 93–94, 108, 234, 245, 258–59, 262–63, 268–69, 290–91; Walliser, "Early Blooming Perennials: 10 Favorites," Savvy Gardening (website).

11. Gardening with Charlie Nardozzi (website), "How to Grow: Chelone" (podcast).

12. Leatherbarrow and Reynolds, *101 Best Plants for the Prairies*, 46–47, 100–101; Macdonald, "How to Grow Hops," West Coast Seeds (website); University of Illinois Extension (website), "Perennial Vines"; Beaulieu, "Jackman's Clematis Plant Profile," The Spruce (website); Beaulieu, "How to Grow and Care for Sweet Autumn Clematis," The Spruce (website).

13. University of California (website), "Safe and Poisonous Garden Plants"; Government of Alberta (website), "Poisonous Outdoor Plants."

Sources

Adamant, Ashley. "Growing Garlic as a Perennial." Practical Self Reliance. August 28, 2018. practicalselfreliance.com/perennial-garlic/.

Agri-Facts. "Rhubarb Production in Alberta." Last updated August 1, 2002. open.alberta.ca/publications/rhubarb-production-in-alberta.

Allonsy, Amelia. "How to Reseed Perennials." SFGATE. Accessed March 31, 2022. homeguides.sfgate.com/reseed-perennials-22889.html.

American Daylily Society. "Gall Midge." Accessed March 31, 2022. daylilies.org /daylily-dictionary/hemerocallis-gall-midge/.

Badgett, Becca. "Sempervivum Is Dying: Fixing Drying Leaves on Hens and Chicks." Gardening Know How. Last updated March 22, 2022. gardeningknowhow .com/ornamental/cacti-succulents/hens-chicks/drying-leaves-on-hens-and-chicks.htm.

————. "Toad Lily Care: Information about the Toad Lily Plant." Gardening Know How. Last updated March 22, 2022. gardeningknowhow.com/ornamental /bulbs/toad-lily/toad-lily-care.htm.

B&D Lilies. "Be Mindful of Lily Bulblets." June 14, 2014. bdlilies.blogspot.com /2014/06/be-mindful-of-lily-bulblets.html.

Barber, Callie. "Characteristics of Shade Plants." SFGATE. Last updated July 21, 2017. homeguides.sfgate.com/characteristics-of-shade-plants-13427210.html.

Beaulieu, David. "How to Grow and Care for Sweet Autumn Clematis." The Spruce. Last updated January 25, 2022. thespruce.com/sweet-autumn -clematis-2132891.

————. "Jackman's Clematis Plant Profile." The Spruce. Last updated October 6, 2020. thespruce.com/jackmans-clematis-vine-4125599.

————. "What Are Herbaceous Plants?" The Spruce. Last updated July 7, 2021. thespruce.com/what-are-herbaceous-plants-2131063.

————. "When to Remove Mulch from Perennials in Spring." The Spruce. Last updated February 3, 2022. thespruce.com/when-to-remove-mulch-for-spring -perennials-2130852.

————. "Why You Should Be Deadheading Plants." The Spruce. Last updated December 7, 2020. thespruce.com/why-you-should-be-deadheading-plants-2132406.

Belgian Nursery. "Growing Perennials in Pots and Planters." Accessed March 31, 2022. belgian-nursery.com/growing-perennials-in-pots-planters/.

Biology Dictionary. "Herbaceous." Accessed March 28, 2022. biologydictionary.net /herbaceous/.

Bloomin Designs Nursery. "The Root of the Perennial Plant." March 8, 2015. bloomindesigns.com/blog/bloomindesigns-449d7c/.

Bradley, Steve. *The Pruner's Bible*. London, UK: Quarto Publishing, 2005.

British Columbia Ministry of Agriculture. "Daylily Hemerocallis Gall Midge." March 2016. gov.bc.ca/assets/gov/farming-natural-resources-and-industry/agriculture -and-seafood/animal-and-crops/plant-health/phu-daylily-gall-midge.pdf.

Brown, Stephen. "Fact Sheet: Anthracnose Disease of Ornamental Plants: A Pictorial." University of Florida. February 3, 2018. blogs.ifas.ufl.edu/leeco/2018 /02/03/factsheet-anthracnose/.

Calgary Gardening. "Planting Asparagus Crowns in Calgary." Accessed March 31, 2022. calgarygardening.ca/planting-asparagus-crowns/.

Cambridge Dictionary. "Perennial." Accessed March 28, 2022. dictionary.cambridge.org/dictionary/english/perennial.

Capon, Brian. *Botany for Gardeners*, 3rd ed. Portland, OR: Timber Press, 2010.

Carroll, Jackie. "Gray Mold Control: Learn about the Treatment of Botrytis Blight." Gardening Know How. Last updated March 22, 2022. gardeningknowhow.com /plant-problems/disease/treating-botrytis-blight.htm.

Connors, Lillian. "Weeding Made Easy: Tips and Tricks." Homesteading.com. Accessed March 31, 2022. homesteading.com/weeding-made-easy-tips-tricks/.

Cook, Hazel. "Dividing Peonies." Canadian Peony Society. June 10, 2012. canadianpeonysociety.blogspot.com/2012/06/dividing-peonies.html.

Dawson, Donna, and Laura Peters. *Perennials for Alberta*. Edmonton: Lone Pine Publishing, 2005.

DeJohn, Suzanne. "Grow Perennials from Seed." Gardener's Supply Company. Accessed March 31, 2022. gardeners.com/how-to/perennials-from-seed /7530.html.

de Long, Eric. "Dividing Perennials." Cornell Cooperative Extension. September 2001. chemung.cce.cornell.edu/resources/dividing-perennials.

Demers, Jill E., Megan K. Romberg, and Lisa A. Castlebury. "Microcyclic Rusts of Hollyhock (*Alcea rosea*)." National Library of Medicine. November 20, 2015. ncbi .nlm.nih.gov/pmc/articles/PMC4681263/.

Downer, A. James, Steven Swain, and Amanda Crump. "Anthracnose." University of California. Accessed March 31, 2022. ipm.ucanr.edu/PMG/PESTNOTES/pn7420 .html.

Dunnett, Nigel. *Naturalistic Planting Design*. London, UK: Filbert Press, 2019.

Engeland, Ron L. *Growing Great Garlic*. Okanogan, WA: Filaree Productions, 1991.

Engels, Jonathan. "Ornamental Plants That Are Edible and/or Edible Plants That Are Ornamental." Permaculture Research Institute. June 23, 2018. permaculturenews.org/2018/06/23/ornamental-plants-edible-edible-plants-ornamental/. .

Espace pour la vie. "Gardening for Biodiversity." Accessed March 30, 2022. espacepourlavie.ca/en/gardening-biodiversity.

———. "Native, Exotic, Naturalized or Invasive." Accessed March 30, 2022. espacepourlavie.ca/en/native-exotic-naturalized-or-invasive.

Fine Gardening. "Six Tips for Effective Weed Control." Accessed March 31, 2022. finegardening.com/project-guides/gardening-basics/six-tips-for-effective-weed-control.

Flanagan, June. Native Plants for Prairie Gardens. Calgary: Fifth House, 2005.

Forney, Julie Martens. "Transplanting Peonies." HGTV. Accessed March 31, 2022. hgtv.com/outdoors/flowers-and-plants/flowers/transplanting-peonies.

———. "When to Divide Perennials." HGTV. Accessed March 31, 2022. hgtv.com/outdoors/gardens/planting-and-maintenance/when-to-divide-perennials.

Gardener's Supply Company. "How to Choose Flower Supports." Last updated January 24, 2021. gardeners.com/how-to/choosing-flower-supports/8196.html.

Garden Gate. "Perennial Seeds to Plant in Fall." Accessed March 31, 2022. gardengatemagazine.com/articles/how-to/start-seeds/perennial-seeds-to-plant-in-fall/.

Gardening with Charlie Nardozzi. "How to Grow: Chelone" (podcast). Accessed April 1, 2022. gardeningwithcharlie.com/how-to-grow-chelone-turltes-head/.

Gardens Illustrated. "Best Plants for Winter Seedheads." Accessed March 31, 2022. gardensillustrated.com/plants/seedheads-for-winter-structure/.

Garland, Lincoln. "Native versus Non-native: Which Plants Are Best for Biodiversity?" The Nature of Cities. May 18, 2020. thenatureofcities.com/2020/05/18/native-versus-non-native-which-plants-are-best-for-biodiversity/.

Gibson, Dianna L. "Red Lily Beetle (Lilioceris lilii)." B&D Lilies. Accessed March 31, 2022. bdlilies.com/redlilybeetle.html.

Government of Alberta. "Poisonous Outdoor Plants." 1995. agric.gov.ab.ca/$Department/deptdocs.nsf/all/agdex13348/$FILE/666-2.pdf.

Government of Canada. "Food Safety Tips for Fiddleheads." Last updated May 6, 2015. canada.ca/en/health-canada/services/food-safety-fruits-vegetables/fiddlehead-safety-tips.html.

———. "Plant Hardiness Zones." December 31, 2010. open.canada.ca/data/en/dataset/db9b4130-8893-11e0-9b96-6cf049291510.

Grant, Bonnie L. "What Is Reseeding: How to Manage Self-Seeders in Gardens." Gardening Know How. Last updated March 22, 2022. gardeningknowhow.com /garden-how-to/propagation/seeds/managing-self-seeders.htm.

Greenshack. "Can Plants Live Forever? (Detailed Explanation)." Accessed March 28, 2022. green-shack.com/can-plants-live-forever/.

Harlequin's Gardens. "Insectary Plants: Let Nature Manage the Pests." Accessed March 31, 2022. harlequinsgardens.com/insectory-plants-let-nature-manage-the-pests/.

Haynes, Cindy. "Cultivar versus Variety." Iowa State University Extension and Outreach. February 6, 2008. hortnews.extension.iastate.edu/2008/2-6/Cultivar OrVariety.html.

Hettinger, Ned. "Conceptualizing and Evaluating Non-native Species." The Nature Knowledge Education Project. 2021. nature.com/scitable/knowledge /library/conceptualizing-and-evaluating-non-native-species-80060037/.

Hidden Habitat Ecological Landscapes. "Benefits of Using Native Plants." Accessed March 31, 2022. hiddenhabitat.ca/benefits-of-using-native-plants/.

Hole, Lois. *Perennial Favorites*. Edmonton: Lone Pine Publishing, 1995.

Hudelson, Brian, and Laura Jull. "Root and Crown Rots." Wisconsin Horticulture. Last updated August 13, 2012. hort.extension.wisc.edu/articles/root-and-crown-rots/.

Hughes, Megan. "How to Save Seeds from Your Garden to Plant Next Year." *Better Homes and Gardens*. August 11, 2020. bhg.com/gardening/yard/garden-care/garden -seed-tips/.

Iannotti, Marie. "10 Aggressively Spreading Plants and How to Deal with Them." The Spruce. Last updated January 10, 2022. thespruce.com/how-to-deal -with-plant-thugs-1403542.

———. "10 Perennial Flowers to Start from Seed." The Spruce. Last updated April 12, 2021. thespruce.com/perennial-flowers-to-start-from-seed-1402891.

Iowa State University. "Hollyhock Rust." Accessed March 31, 2022. hortnews.extension.iastate.edu/hollyhock-rust.

———. "Is It Safe to Eat Rhubarb after the Plants Have Been Exposed to Freezing Temperatures?" Accessed March 31, 2022. hortnews.extension.iastate.edu/faq/it-safe -eat-rhubarb-after-plants-have-been-exposed-freezing-temperatures.

———. "When Can I Cut Back My Asparagus Foliage?" Accessed March 31, 2022. hortnews.extension.iastate.edu/faq/when-can-i-cut-back-my-asparagus-foliage.

Jabbour, Niki. "Collecting Seeds from Your Garden." Savvy Gardening. Accessed March 31, 2022. savvygardening.com/collecting-seeds-from-your-garden/.

Jauron, Richard. "Perennials with Colorful Foliage." Iowa State University. April 25, 1997. hortnews.extension.iastate.edu/1997/4-25-1997/colorfulperen.html.

Johnny's Selected Seeds. "Plants for Insectaries." Accessed March 31, 2022. johnnyseeds.com/growers-library/farm-seed-cover-crops/insectary-plantings.html.

Johnson, Tim. "Fall Is a Great Time to Divide Perennials, but Don't Wait Too Long." *Chicago Tribune.* September 28, 2015. chicagotribune.com/lifestyles/home-and-garden/ct-garden-divide-perennials-home-qa-1001-20150928-story.html.

Johnstone, Gemma. "How to Grow Gas Plants." The Spruce. Last updated March 15, 2021. thespruce.com/gas-plant-plant-care-5081295.

Kelaidis, Panayoti. "10 Perennials Easily Grown from Seed." *Fine Gardening.* Accessed March 31, 2022. finegardening.com/project-guides/gardening-basics/10-perennials-easily-grown-from-seed.

Kelsey, Anni. *Edible Perennial Gardening.* East Meon, Hampshire, UK: Permanent Publications, 2014.

Knauss, Nancy, and Pamela T. Hubbard. "Cutting Down Perennials in the Fall." PennState Extension. October 18, 2016. extension.psu.edu/cutting-down-perennials-in-the-fall.

Laidback Gardener. "Head in the Sun, Feet in the Shade." June 26, 2015. laidbackgardener.blog/2015/06/26/head-in-the-sun-feet-in-the-shade/.

Landscape Ontario. "Perennials for Your Rock Garden." June 3, 2013. landscapeontario.com/perennials-for-your-rock-garden.

Leatherbarrow, Liesbeth, and Lesley Reynolds. *101 Best Plants for the Prairies.* Calgary: Fifth House, 1999.

Lerner, Rosie. "Rhubarb Flowers Blooming or Bolting?" Purdue University. Accessed March 31, 2022. purdue.edu/hla/sites/yardandgarden/rhubarb-flowers-blooming-or-bolting/.

Lewis, Penny. "Where the Wild Things Are: How to Support Wildlife in the Modern Gardening World." Ecological Landscape Alliance. February 17, 2014. ecolandscaping.org/02/designing-ecological-landscapes/native-plants/where-the-wild-things-are-how-to-support-wildlife-in-the-modern-gardening-world/.

Lima, Patrick. *The Perennial Garden.* Toronto: Camden House Publishing, 1987.

Lorecentral. "Advantages and Disadvantages of Hybridization in Plants." Accessed March 29, 2022. lorecentral.org/2018/03/advantages-and-disadvantages-of-hybridization-in-plants.html.

Loughrey, Janet. "Heuchera—the Ultimate Guide to Coral Bells from Proven Winners." Proven Winners. Accessed March 31, 2022. provenwinners.com/learn/heuchera.

Macdonald, Mark. "How to Grow Hops." West Coast Seeds. February 12, 2015. westcoastseeds.com/blogs/how-to-grow/grow-hops.

Mahr, Susan. "Sea Thrift, *Armeria maritima*." Wisconsin Horticulture. Accessed April 1, 2022. hort.extension.wisc.edu/articles/sea-thrift-armeria-maritima/.

Martin, Susan. "Native Species or Cultivars of Native Plants." Piedmont Master Gardeners. July 2020. piedmontmastergardeners.org/article/native-species-or -cultivars-of-native-plants-does-it-matter/.

Masterclass. "How to Grow Candytuft Flowers: 5 Care Tips for Candytufts." Last updated February 24, 2022. masterclass.com/articles/candytuft-plant-care-guide.

Michigan State University. "Botrytis Blight." Accessed March 31, 2022. canr.msu .edu/resources/botrytis-blight.

Millcreek Nursery Ltd. "Hillside Black Beauty Bugbane." Accessed April 1, 2022. search.millcreeknursery.ca/11050005/Plant/3420/Hillside_Black_Beauty_Bugbane/.

Missouri Botanical Garden. "Botrytis Blight." Accessed March 31, 2022. missouribotanicalgarden.org/gardens-gardening/your-garden/help-for-the-home -gardener/advice-tips-resources/pests-and-problems/diseases/fungal-spots/botrytis -blight.aspx.

———. "Bud-Blast of Peony." Accessed March 31, 2022. missouribotanicalgarden .org/gardens-gardening/your-garden/help-for-the-home-gardener/advice-tips -resources/pests-and-problems/environmental/bud-blast.aspx.

———. "Clematis Wilt." Accessed March 31, 2022. missouribotanicalgarden.org /gardens-gardening/your-garden/help-for-the-home-gardener/advice-tips-resources /pests-and-problems/diseases/cankers/clematis-wilt.aspx.

———. "Root, Stem, Crown, and Collar Rot." Accessed March 31, 2022. missouribotanicalgarden.org/gardens-gardening/your-garden/help-for-the-home -gardener/advice-tips-resources/pests-and-problems/diseases/rot.aspx.

———. "Rust of Hollyhock." Accessed March 31, 2022. missouribotanicalgarden .org/gardens-gardening/your-garden/help-for-the-home-gardener/advice-tips -resources/pests-and-problems/diseases/rusts/rust-of-hollyhock.aspx.

Mother Earth News. "Organic Pest Control: The Best Plants to Attract Beneficial Insects and Bees." May 19, 2010. motherearthnews.com/organic-gardening/plants-to -attract-beneficial-insects-zl0z1005zvau/.

Murphy, Sharon Wallish. "How to Get Rid of Delphinium Worms." Gardening with Sharon. June 2, 2021. gardeningwithsharon.com/growing-perennials/how-to -get-rid-of-delphinium-worms/.

Myers, Melinda. "Managing Self-Seeding Perennials." Accessed March 31, 2022. melindamyers.com/audio-video/melindas-garden-moment-audio-tips/flowers -ornamental-grasses/managing-self-seeding-perennials.

———. "What to Do with Asiatic Lily Seed Pods." Accessed March 31, 2022. melindamyers.com/articles/what-to-do-with-asiatic-lily-seed-pods.

National Gardening Association. "Terminology: Genus and Species." 1999. garden.org/courseweb/course1/week3/page3.htm.

Neveln, Viveka. "Staking and Training Perennials." *Better Homes and Gardens*. May 6, 2016. bhg.com/gardening/flowers/perennials/staking-and-training-perennials/.

Neverman, Laurie. "Before You Plant Sunchokes, You Need to Read This Post." Common Sense Home. Last updated January 18, 2017. commonsensehome.com /before-you-plant-sunchokes/.

Olds College. "The Lily Beetle." Accessed March 31, 2022. oldscollege.ca/about /campus/botanic-gardens/central-gardens/taxonomic-collection/the-lily-beetle/index.html.

Oregon State University. "Perennials: How to Dig and Divide!" Accessed March 31, 2022. extension.oregonstate.edu/gardening/flowers-shrubs-trees/perennials-how-dig-divide.

Ostrich Ferns. "Ostrich Ferns." Accessed March 31, 2022. ostrichferns.com.

Pacific Northwest Pest Management Handbooks. "Clematis—Leaf and Stem Spot." Accessed March 31, 2022. pnwhandbooks.org/plantdisease/host-disease/clematis -leaf-stem-spot.

————. "Rhubarb (*Rheum rhabarbarum*)—Red Leaf." Accessed March 31, 2022. pnwhandbooks.org/plantdisease/host-disease/rhubarb-rheum-rhabarbarum-red-leaf.

Paraspace. "Plant Hardiness Zones in Canada: How Do They Work?" April 3, 2021. paraspaceinc.com/blog/plant-hardiness-zones.

Passiglia's Nursery and Garden Center. "What to Do When Your Perennials Don't Come Up." Accessed March 31, 2022. passiglia.com/what-to-do-when-your -perennials-dont-come-up/.

Patterson, Susan. "Invasive Plant List: Learn about What Plants Are Aggressive." Gardening Know How. Last updated March 22, 2022. gardeningknowhow.com /plant-problems/weeds/aggressive-garden-plants.htm.

————. "Seed Stratification: What Seeds Require Cold Treatment." Gardening Know How. Last updated March 22, 2022. gardeningknowhow.com/garden-how-to /propagation/seeds/seed-stratification.htm.

Pearman, Myrna, and Ted Pike. *NatureScape Alberta*. Edmonton: Red Deer River Naturalists and Federation of Alberta Naturalists, 2000.

Perennials.com. "Saving and Starting Perennials Seeds." Accessed March 31, 2022. perennials.com/content/saving-and-starting-perennials-seeds/.

Planet Natural Research Center. "Anthracnose." Accessed March 31, 2022. planetnatural.com/pest-problem-solver/plant-disease/anthracnose/.

Plant Perfect. "'Tender Perennials You Can Keep as Houseplants Over Winter.'" Accessed March 31, 2022. plantperfect.com/tender-perennials-you-can-keep-as -houseplants-over-winter/.

Post Bulletin. "Growing Concerns: Root Systems Have a Role to Play in Plant Division." September 15, 2018. postbulletin.com/lifestyle/growing-concerns-root -systems-have-a-role-to-play-in-plant-division.

Prairie Originals. "Wildflowers for Dry to Medium Soil." Accessed March 31, 2022. prairieoriginals.com/index.php?page=dry-to-medium.

Proven Winners. "What Does Full Sun or Part Shade Mean?" Accessed March 31, 2022. provenwinners.com/learn/finding-right-plant/what-does-full-sun-or-part-shade-mean.

Rainer, Thomas, and Claudia West. *Planting in a Post-Wild World.* Portland, OR: Timber Press, 2015.

Rayment, Barbara. *The Northern Gardener.* Madeira Park, BC: Harbour Publishing Co. Ltd., 2012.

Regina Gardening Associates Inc. "Perennial Flowers for Partial Sun to Full Sun." Accessed March 31, 2022. reginafloralconservatory.ca/wp-content/uploads/2013/07 /RGA_FactSheets_SunPerennials_web.pdf.

Restoration Seeds. "Germinating Perennial Seeds." Accessed March 31, 2022. restorationseeds.com/blogs/news/7211932-germinating-perennial-seeds.

Rhoades, Heather. "Cutting Asparagus Foliage Back in Autumn." Gardening Know How. Last updated March 22, 2022. gardeningknowhow.com/edible/vegetables /asparagus/cutting-asparagus-foliage-back-in-autumn.htm.

———. "Growing Horseradish: How to Grow Horseradish." Gardening Know How. Last updated March 22, 2022. gardeningknowhow.com/edible/herbs /horseradish/growing-horseradish-how-to-grow-horseradish.htm.

Rhoades, Jackie. "False Indigo Growing Tips: Growing and Caring for Baptisia Plants." Gardening Know How. Last updated on March 22, 2022. gardeningknowhow.com/ornamental/flowers/baptisia/growing-baptisia-plants.htm.

Riordan, Katie Avis, and Steven Robinson. "Top Tips for a Biodiverse Garden." Royal Botanic Gardens Kew. May 30, 2020. kew.org/read-and-watch/how-to-make -your-garden-more-biodiverse.

Salisbury Greenhouse. "8 Great Groundcovers for Zone 3 Gardens." Accessed April 1, 2022. salisburygreenhouse.com/8-great-groundcovers-for-zone-3-gardens/.

———. "How to Grow Your Favourite Perennials from Seed." Accessed March 31, 2022. salisburygreenhouse.com/how-to-grow-your-favourite-perennials-from-seed/.

———. "How to Move Plants Indoors for Winter." Accessed March 31, 2022. salisburygreenhouse.com/how-to-move-plants-indoors-for-the-winter/.

Schmidt, Katie. "Coneflowers: Native vs Hybrid." Dyck Arboretum. July 15, 2018. dyckarboretum.org/coneflowers-native-hybrid/.

Scholtens, Peter. "Why Grow Native Plants?" Canadian Wildlife Federation. Accessed March 31, 2022. cwf-fcf.org/en/news/articles/why-grow-native-plants.html.

Science and Plants for Schools. "Some Physical Differences between Sun and Shade Plants." Accessed March 31, 2022. saps.org.uk/saps-associates/browse-q-and -a/158-q-a-a-what-is-the-physical-difference-between-plants-that-grow-in-the-direct -sunlight-and-those-that-grow-in-the-shade.

Shakespeare, William. *Romeo and Juliet.* In *The Globe Illustrated Shakespeare.* Edited by Howard Staunton. New York: Greenwich House, 1986.

Shaw, Hank. "The Bracken Fern: A Natural Born Killer?" *The Atlantic.* June 30, 2011. theatlantic.com/health/archive/2011/06/the-bracken-fern-a-natural-born -killer/241271/.

Shinn, Meghan. "Forbs: What Is a Forb?" *Horticulture.* October 25, 2011. hortmag .com/weekly-tips/forbs.

Siegel, Julie. "Design Theory: How Many Plants Do You Need?" *Fine Gardening.* Accessed March 30, 2022. finegardening.com/project-guides/gardening-basics/plant -by-number.

Smith, Miranda. *The Plant Propagator's Bible.* London, UK: Quarto Publishing, 2007.

Smith, Tina. "Lily Leaf Beetle." University of Massachusetts Amherst. Last updated 2013. ag.umass.edu/greenhouse-floriculture/fact-sheets/lily-leaf-beetle.

Spengler, Teo. "Problems with Peonies: Reasons Peony Buds Don't Develop." Gardening Know How. Last updated March 22, 2022. gardeningknowhow.com /ornamental/flowers/peony/peony-bud-blast.htm.

Sproule, Rob. "Growing Asparagus in Alberta." Salisbury Greenhouse. Accessed March 31, 2022. salisburygreenhouse.com/growing-asparagus-in-alberta/.

Stevenson, Lorraine. "Frost-Touched Rhubarb Can Be Poisonous." *Manitoba Co-operator.* May 28, 2015. manitobacooperator.ca/news-opinion/news/local/frost -touched-rhubarb-can-be-poisonous/.

Sweetser, Robin. "How to Bring Outdoor Plants Indoors." *The Old Farmer's Almanac.* September 22, 2021. almanac.com/how-bring-outdoor-plants-indoors.

———. "How to Cut Back Perennials in Fall." *The Old Farmer's Almanac.* September 20, 2021. almanac.com/how-cut-back-perennials-fall.

Tangren, Dr. Sara. "Cultivars of Native Plants." University of Maryland Extension. Last updated April 20, 2021. extension.umd.edu/resource/cultivars-native-plants.

Tannas, Kathy. *Common Plants of the Western Rangelands*, vol 3. Edmonton: Alberta Agriculture and Rural Development, 2004.

Thomson, Julie R. "What Exactly IS Rhubarb, Anyway?" HuffPost. Last updated February 11, 2021. huffpost.com/entry/what-is-rhubarb-fruit-or-vegetable_n_7534888.

Tilley, Nikki. "Crown Rot Identification and Tips for Crown Rot Treatment." Gardening Know How. Last updated March 22, 2022. gardeningknowhow.com /plant-problems/disease/crown-rot-disease.htm.

———. "Deadheading Flowers: Encouraging a Second Bloom in the Garden." Gardening Know How. Last updated March 22, 2022. gardeningknowhow.com /ornamental/flowers/fgen/deadheading-flowers.htm.

Toop, Edgar, and Sara Williams. *Perennials for the Prairies*. Edmonton: University of Alberta Faculty of Extension, 1991.

Toronto Master Gardeners. "Determining Sun Quality." Accessed March 31, 2022. torontomastergardeners.ca/askagardener/determining-sun-quality/.

Uelmen, Nicole. "Hollyhock Rust." Wisconsin Horticulture Division of Extension. Last updated March 6, 2014. hort.extension.wisc.edu/articles/hollyhock-rust/.

University of California. "Insectary Plants." Accessed March 31, 2022. ipm.ucanr .edu/mitigation/insectary_plants.html.

———. "Safe and Poisonous Garden Plants." Accessed April 1, 2022. ucanr.edu /sites/poisonous_safe_plants/Toxic_Plants_by_common_Name_659/.

University of Illinois Extension. "Gardening with Perennials: After Planting Care." Accessed March 31, 2022. web.extension.illinois.edu/perennials/care.cfm.

———."Perennial Vines." Accessed April 1, 2022. web.extension.illinois.edu/vines /perennials.cfm.

University of New Hampshire. "What Is the Best Way to Deadhead Perennials?" July 12, 2019. extension.unh.edu/blog/2019/07/what-best-way-deadhead-perennials.

———. " When Should I Divide My Perennials?" March 18, 2021. extension.unh .edu/blog/2021/03/when-should-i-divide-my-perennials.

University of Saskatchewan. "Creating Biodiversity in Your Yard." February 2, 2018. gardening.usask.ca/articles-and-lists/articles-how-to/creating-biodiversity-in-your-yard.php.

———. "Delphinium Worm." January 29, 2018. gardening.usask.ca/articles-and -lists/articles-insects/article-delphinium-worm.php.

Vale's Greenhouse. "Alpine Garden." Accessed April 1, 2022. valesgreenhouse.com /alpine_garden_article.html.

Valleau, John. "Dividing Perennials in the Spring." Perennials.com. Accessed March 31, 2022. perennials.com/content/dividing-perennials-in-the-spring/.

Walliser, Jessica. "Early Blooming Perennials: 10 Favorites." Savvy Gardening. Accessed April 1, 2022. savvygardening.com/10-favorite-early-blooming-perennials/.

———. "Evergreen Groundcover Plants: 20 Choices for Year-Round Interest." Savvy Gardening. Accessed April 1, 2022. savvygardening.com/evergreen -groundcover/.

———. "Shade-Loving Perennial Flowers: 15 Beautiful Choices." Savvy Gardening. Accessed March 31, 2022. savvygardening.com/shade-loving-perennial -flowers/.

Walters Gardens. "The Complete Guide to Growing Perennials in Containers." October 7, 2014. waltersgardens.com/article.php?ID=109.

Watson, Molly, and Danilo Alfaro. "What Are Fiddlehead Ferns?" The Spruce Eats. Last updated December 9, 2021. thespruceeats.com/all-about-fiddlehead -ferns-2217471.

Weigel, George. "Do Perennial Flowers Need to Be Covered If There Is a Frost." PennLive.com. Last updated January 5, 2019. pennlive.com/gardening /2015/04/do_perennial_flowers_need_to_b.html.

Weisenhorn, Julie, and Molly Furgeson. "How and When to Divide Perennials." University of Minnesota Extension. 2019. extension.umn.edu/planting-and-growing -guides/dividing-perennials.

Wild about Flowers. "Browse by Latin Name." Accessed April 1, 2022. wildaboutflowers.ca/browse_latin_plant_name.php.

Wildfong, Bob. "Stratification for Dormant Seeds." Seeds of Diversity. March 2016. seeds.ca/d/?t=06c683b400002950.

Will, Melissa J. "25 Annual and Perennial Flower Seeds to Sow in Fall." Empress of Dirt. Last updated October 24, 2021. empressofdirt.net/sow-fall-flower-seeds/.

Wilson, Catherine. "9 Beautiful Edible Ornamental Plants." Grow Network. December 19, 2020. thegrownetwork.com/edible-ornamental-plants/.

Index

Page numbers in italics refer to photographs.

NOTES

NOTES

© Steve Melrose

About the Authors

SHERYL NORMANDEAU was born and raised in the Peace Country region of northern Alberta and has made Calgary her home since 1994. A writer and master gardener, Sheryl holds a bachelor's degree in English as well as a Prairie Horticulture Certificate and an Urban Sustainable Agriculture Certificate. Since 2013, she has served as the online Ask an Expert for the Calgary Horticultural Society. She works at the Calgary Public Library—besides gardening, books of all kinds are her grand passion! She is a small-space gardener (on a tiny balcony and in a plot in a nearby community garden) and she is most enthusiastic about growing veggies. She lives with her husband, Rob, and their rescue cat Smudge. Find Sheryl at Flowery Prose (floweryprose.com) and on Facebook (@FloweryProse), Twitter (@Flowery_Prose), and Instagram (flowery_prose).

JANET MELROSE was born in Trinidad, West Indies, and immigrated to Canada in 1964. She has lived in Calgary since 1969. She is a master gardener and the creator and owner of the successful horticulture business Calgary's Cottage Gardener, which specializes in garden education and consultation, horticultural therapy, and advocating for sustainable local food systems. She holds bachelor's degrees in sociology and history, a Prairie Horticulture Certificate, and a Horticultural Therapy Certificate. Janet is a lifelong gardener, coming from a heritage of English gardening. She has a large garden at home in the suburbs of Calgary that can only be described as a typical cottage garden. She cares for many other gardens throughout Calgary through her work as a horticultural therapist as well as a bed at the Inglewood Community Garden. She is married to Steve and has two children, Jennifer and David. Three cats, Patrick, Theo, and Mia, currently own their home and patrol against the deer, hares, squirrels, skunk, mice, insects and assorted birds that believe the garden is theirs, too! Connect with Janet on Facebook (@Calgarys-Cottage-Gardener), Twitter (@CalCottageGrdnr), and Instagram (CalgarysCottageGardener).

About the Series

It looks like you've discovered the Guides for the Prairie Gardener! This budding series puts the combined knowledge of two lifelong prairie gardeners at your grubby fingertips. Whether you've just cleared a few square feet for your first bed of veggies or are a seasoned green thumb stumped by that one cultivar you can't seem to master, we think you'll find Janet and Sheryl the ideal teachers. Find answers on seeds, soil, trees, flowers, weather, climate, pests, pots, and quite a few more. These slim but mighty volumes, handsomely designed, make great companions at the height of summer in the garden trenches and during cold winter days planning the next season. With regional expertise, elegance, and a sense of humour, Janet and Sheryl take your questions and turn them into prairie gardening inspiration. For more information, and for other titles in the series, visit touchwoodeditions.com/guidesprairiegardener.